GUID

May–August 2022

Edited by **Helen Paynter**, **Rachel Tranter** and **Olivia Warburton**

15 The Chambers, Vineyard
Abingdon OX14 3FE
brf.org.uk

Bible Reading Fellowship is a charity (233280)
and company limited by guarantee (301324),
registered in England and Wales

ISBN 978 1 80039 122 2
All rights reserved

This edition © Bible Reading Fellowship 2022
Cover image © agsandrew/stock.adobe.com

Distributed in Australia by:
MediaCom Education Inc, PO Box 610, Unley, SA 5061
Tel: 1 800 811 311 | admin@mediacom.org.au

Distributed in New Zealand by:
Scripture Union Wholesale, PO Box 760, Wellington
Tel: 04 385 0421 | suwholesale@clear.net.nz

Acknowledgements
Scripture quotations marked with the following acronyms are taken from the
version shown. Where no acronym is given, the quotation is taken from the version
stated in the contributor's introduction. NRSV: The New Revised Standard Version
of the Bible, Anglicised edition, copyright © 1989, 1995 by the Division of Christian
Education of the National Council of the Churches of Christ in the United States
of America. Used by permission. All rights reserved. NIV: The Holy Bible, New
International Version (Anglicised edition) copyright © 1979, 1984, 2011 by Biblica.
Used by permission of Hodder & Stoughton Publishers, a Hachette UK company.
All rights reserved. 'NIV' is a registered trademark of Biblica. UK trademark number
1448790. ESV: The Holy Bible, English Standard Version, published by HarperCollins
Publishers, © 2001 Crossway Bibles, a division of Good News Publishers. Used
by permission. All rights reserved. KJV: The Authorised Version of the Bible (The
King James Bible), the rights in which are vested in the Crown, are reproduced by
permission of the Crown's Patentee, Cambridge University Press.

Every effort has been made to trace and contact copyright owners for material used
in this resource. We apologise for any inadvertent omissions or errors, and would
ask those concerned to contact us so that full acknowledgement can be made in
the future.

A catalogue record for this book is available from the British Library

Printed by Gutenberg Press, Tarxien, Malta

Suggestions for using *Guidelines*

Set aside a regular time and place, if possible, when and where you can read and pray undisturbed. Before you begin, take time to be still and, if you find it helpful, use one of the BRF prayers on page 6.

In *Guidelines*, the introductory section provides context for the passages or themes to be studied, while the units of comment can be used daily, weekly or whatever best fits your timetable. You will need a Bible (more than one if you want to compare different translations) as Bible passages are not included. Please don't be tempted to skip the Bible reading because you know the passage well. We will have utterly failed if we don't bring our readers into engagement with the word of God. At the end of each week is a 'Guidelines' section, offering further thoughts about or practical application of what you have been studying.

Occasionally, you may read something in *Guidelines* that you find particularly challenging, even uncomfortable. This is inevitable in a series of notes which draws on a wide spectrum of contributors and doesn't believe in ducking difficult issues. Indeed, we believe that *Guidelines* readers much prefer thought-provoking material to a bland diet that only confirms what they already think.

If you do disagree with a contributor, you may find it helpful to go through these three steps. First, think about why you feel uncomfortable. Perhaps this is an idea that is new to you, or you are not happy about the way something has been expressed. Or there may be something more substantial – you may feel that the writer is guilty of sweeping generalisation, factual error, or theological or ethical misjudgement. Second, pray that God would use this disagreement to teach you more about his word and about yourself. Third, have a deeper read about the issue. There are further reading suggestions at the end of each writer's block of notes. And then, do feel free to write to the contributor or the editor of *Guidelines*. We welcome communication, by email, phone or letter, as it enables us to discover what has been useful, challenging or infuriating for our readers. We don't always promise to change things, but we will always listen and think about your ideas, complaints or suggestions. Thank you!

To send feedback, please email **enquiries@brf.org.uk**, phone **+44 (0)1865 319700** or write to the address shown opposite.

Writers in this issue

Steve Walton is associate research fellow and part-time tutor in New Testament at Trinity College, Bristol. He is a retired international volleyball referee and lives in west London with his wife Ali, a vicar, and their Border Terrier, Flora.

Russell Herbert is a Methodist minister in Clevedon, North Somerset. He has written several books, including *Growing through the Church* (Kevin Mayhew, 2012), *Living Hope* (Kevin Mayhew, 2014) and *Halfway Home? Finding faith in mid-life* (Kevin Mayhew, 2019).

Freddy Hedley is dean of undergraduate studies at Westminster Theological Centre, where he also teaches Old Testament studies. He is a regular speaker at churches and events and has authored several books, including *The God of Page One* (Emblem Books, 2012) and *The Colossian Image* (Alderway, 2016).

Nigel G. Wright is a pastor, theologian, author and lecturer and is principal emeritus of Spurgeon's College and a former president of the Baptist Union of Great Britain. He has been married to Judy for a very long time and they have two children and three grandchildren. They now live in Cheshire. Nigel is currently a visiting professor at the Estonian Free Church Theological Academy.

Ashley Hibbard is a research associate at the Centre for the Study of Bible and Violence, and an adjunct lecturer at African Christian College, Eswatini, and Emmanuel Bible College, Kitchener, Canada.

Gareth Black is a Bible teacher and evangelist with Solas (Centre for Public Christianity), based in Belfast. Beyond biblical studies, he has an academic interest in medical ethics and is currently pursuing a doctorate in end-of-life ethics at the University of Oxford.

Richard Briggs is the prior of the Community of St Cuthbert based at St Nic's Church in the centre of Durham City. He taught Old Testament in Cranmer Hall, Durham, for 18 years.

Terry Griffith has recently retired after 40 years in Baptist ministry, having served in two London pastorates in Hackney and Bexleyheath. Also an associate research fellow at Spurgeon's College, his research has focused on the gospel and letters of John.

Isabelle Hamley is currently theological adviser to the House of Bishops (Church of England), after being chaplain to the Archbishop of Canterbury, a vicar, a theological college lecturer and a university chaplain. She loves the Old Testament and making it relevant to contemporary life.

Helen Paynter writes...

I begin with some personal news. When I took on the editing of *Guidelines* about three years ago, I was working a portfolio role and had easy capacity for this important work. A year ago, I was appointed full-time as tutor at Bristol Baptist College, and in addition, the Centre for the Study of Bible and Violence, which I set up and direct, has really taken off. As a result, my capacity for other things is limited, and I have decided to step back from my role as commissioning editor of *Guidelines*.

I do this with reluctance and with sadness. I hugely appreciate the gifted, learned and dedicated people who contribute reflections week by week. It's a privilege to have worked with them in producing the notes. I often think that writing and editing notes brings the greater blessing, but I do hope that the notes I have had a hand in shaping have been a blessing to you, our readers.

I am delighted that Olivia Warburton and Rachel Tranter of BRF have agreed to take over the role that I am leaving. They're both very experienced editors, and having worked with them for some time I know of their passion for seeing God's word set free to challenge and inspire.

Speaking of challenging and inspiring, let me preview what we have on offer for you in this edition. I'm delighted to be able to introduce several new writers to you. I heard Gareth Black present on 1 Peter at a conference, and I was so impressed that I invited him to write some notes for us. I had the privilege of sharing the supervision of Ashley Hibbard's PhD thesis on Genesis and Deuteronomy, and I'm delighted that she will be writing on the second half of Genesis for us. Isabelle Hamley has recently published a commentary on Judges, and I'm thrilled that she has written two weeks of notes on that book for us. I'd also like to introduce Freddy Hedley, of Westminster Theological Centre, who is writing on Pentecost. Finally, Methodist minister Russell Herbert, who has recently written a book on the subject, will be taking us through another of life's milestones: middle age.

Of course we have some familiar faces as well. Steve Walton will be taking us on a deep dive into 1 Thessalonians, and Terry Griffith will be studying characters in the fourth gospel. Nigel Wright has two weeks of notes on Trinity, to coincide with Trinity Sunday, and Richard Briggs is leading us through the first part of Exodus.

I pray that these notes will be valuable to you, and that you will experience every joy as you continue to study God's wonderful word.

The BRF Prayer

Almighty God,
you have taught us that your word is a lamp for our feet
and a light for our path. Help us, and all who prayerfully
read your word, to deepen our fellowship with you
and with each other through your love.
And in so doing may we come to know you more fully,
love you more truly, and follow more faithfully
in the steps of your son Jesus Christ, who lives and reigns
with you and the Holy Spirit, one God forevermore.
Amen

The BRF Centenary Prayer

Gracious God,
We rejoice in this centenary year
that you have grown BRF
from a local network of Bible readers
into a worldwide family of ministries.
Thank you for your faithfulness
in nurturing small beginnings
into surprising blessings.
We rejoice that, from the youngest to the oldest,
so many have encountered your word
and grown as disciples of Christ.
Keep us humble in your service,
ambitious for your glory
and open to new opportunities.
For your name's sake
Amen

See page 160 to find out more about BRF's centenary celebrations.

1 Thessalonians

Steve Walton

The church in Thessalonica began when the mission team of Paul, Silas and Timothy visited in the early 50s AD (Acts 17:1–15). This Roman city was prominent in the province of Macedonia (in the north of modern Greece) and was the team's first stop after leaving Philippi, where Paul and Silas had been imprisoned (Acts 16). It was a city where religious competition featured, with temples to the Greek and Roman gods, devotion to the emperor and a Jewish synagogue. The wider culture involved seeking to be 'one up' on others, gaining social status and prominence.

Following Paul's usual approach, they went first to the synagogue, where Paul spoke from the scriptures in order to show that Jesus was the Messiah of Israel. This lasted only three sabbath days, when the synagogue met, before some Jews caused a riot against the missionaries. Before that happened, some Jews and non-Jews had become believers in Jesus, both men and women (Acts 17:4). So the team had to abandon this new church in its infancy, and went away to pray for them and to wonder how they were doing.

Eventually, Paul – by now in Athens – decided he must find out what was going on, so he sent Timothy to visit (1 Thessalonians 3:1–2). The news of the believers was good (3:6), even though they were suffering for their faith, and the team wrote this letter to encourage and strengthen the believers in the light of Timothy's report. Look out for issues of keeping the faith amid persecution, the model of Christian living which the missionaries provided – not giving in to the pagan culture of the city – sexual purity and the Lord's return: the issues Timothy must have reported.

Unless otherwise stated, Bible quotations are taken from the NIV.

1 Beginning at the beginning

1 Thessalonians 1:1

The three writers begin their letter in usual Greek letter style: senders, recipients and greeting. Each has something important to say about the letter and their relationships

'Paul, Silas and Timothy' are the team who planted the church in Thessalonica in a relatively brief visit (Acts 17:1–10 – do stop and read this). At the time of writing, Paul is an experienced missionary of some 15 years' standing as a Christian. He earlier served in Galatia (southern Turkey) and recently went through northern Greece, including Thessalonica. Silas (sometimes Silvanus) is a Jewish-Christian leader with prophetic gifts, trusted by the Jerusalem believers. He worked alongside Paul in Syrian Antioch (Acts 15:22, 27, 32) and was Paul's chosen colleague after Paul and Barnabas separated (Acts 15:36–40). Timothy is a young believer who joins Paul in Lystra, one of the Galatian churches. His mother is a Jewish believer, and Paul arranged for him to be circumcised in order for Timothy to be acceptable among Jews (Acts 16:1–3). Timothy was recently in the city and brought news of the believers there (1 Thessalonians 3:1–2, 6). The team are responding to this news, which includes some concerns relayed by Timothy (see the introduction).

The recipients are a community belonging to God as known in Jesus. That is the most significant thing the writers can say about them: their identity and security are rooted in their relationship with God and his Messiah. Although they live in a particular earthly city, that's not their true home. Paul portrays them as living 'in' God and Jesus – they are now 'at home' with God.

The greeting/prayer-wish of 'grace and peace' for the hearers uses two central Pauline themes. 'Grace' is God's generous and transformative love in Jesus Christ which brings undeserving people to himself through Christ's death (e.g. Romans 6:14). 'Peace' is not like the peace brutally imposed by the Roman military machine, but peace with and from God, a God who offers reconciliation to those who trust Christ (Romans 5:1). These are not just 'nice words', but crucial to the believers grasping their security in what God has done and is doing for them in Jesus.

2 Thanksgiving for God's people

Thanksgiving for the recipients is a feature of Paul's letters – the only exception is Galatians. Often the opening thanksgiving mentions key themes which the letter will develop. It's easy to neglect giving thanks to God because we're thinking about the next thing to do. So it's striking that Paul, Silas and Timothy not only give thanks, but also ensure the believers *know* that they give thanks for them. They tell the Thessalonian Christians that they are an encouragement to them, and why.

Here, the three writers give thanks for the way the faith of the believers is being worked out in their lives (v. 3) and for their memories of their visit to Thessalonica (vv. 4–5).

The writers give thanks particularly for the lifestyle which flows from the Thessalonians' commitment to Christ. This involves their work and labour (v. 3), their readiness to live and act in different ways because they now belong to Jesus. Most English versions translate the phrase as 'work of [or 'produced by'] faith'; the sense of 'faith' here is most probably 'loyalty' or 'trust'. The team commend them here not for *what* they believe, but for their wholehearted loyalty to Christ or trust in him – this is something seen in their lives, for it produces 'work'. Likewise, their love for Christ produces 'labour', actions in service of Jesus and of other people, especially other believers.

Further, their hope in Christ produces 'steadfastness' or 'endurance' – they are hanging on in what could be a tough place to be a follower of Jesus. 'Hope' is not just wishful thinking, 'I hope so,' but Christian confidence about the future based on the promise God has made in Christ. 'Hope' means a focused faith which looks forward. Because of the confidence about the future which believers have, we can live in the present in line with the way the world will be when Christ returns.

Looking back to the planting of the church in Thessalonica, the writers are confident of God's commitment to the believers (v. 4) because of the way the gospel message took effect in their lives (v. 5). It was not mere words which stirred emotions, but words spoken with power through the Holy Spirit. As in Galatia, remarkable events probably took place, 'signs and wonders', as Acts calls them (see Galatians 3:1–5). Not only that, but the hearers were deeply convinced of the gospel's truth, so they responded gladly to it.

3 Self-reproducing models

How does anyone learn the Christian faith and the way of life which goes with it? They learn it from those who were believers before them, and that's why the writers here say that the Thessalonians imitated 'us and… the Lord' (v. 6). They copied the faith and lifestyle they saw in Paul, Silas and Timothy, which was itself modelled on the Lord, Jesus himself. This was transformative: they 'became' imitators – their lives were changed by the gospel message and their encounter with God through this mission team. 2:1–12 unpacks this further and reminds the recipients that their transformation happened through close contact and genuine care between the missionaries and their hearers – to love people and to share the gospel with them involves sharing your life too (2:8).

Having good models to learn from is vital, but especially so when you face attacks on your faith, as these believers did (v. 6). Persecution came from their fellow-citizens (2:14), and probably included being publicly criticised, being excluded from invitations to meals in others' homes or among trade associations, having fellow-citizens refusing to buy from believers' shops or food outlets and other kinds of social exclusion. Paul himself was so concerned about the persecution they faced that he was ready to be alone in Athens in order to send Timothy to find out how they were doing and to encourage them in their suffering for Jesus (3:1–3).

Remarkably, not only did they endure this suffering, but they did it with joy which the Holy Spirit gave them (v. 6). Their surrender to Christ meant they experienced human life as it is meant to be lived, in the presence of God and as an experience of God – and that produced great joy. The earliest Christians showed great joy in the face of suffering because what they knew in Christ filled their lives to bursting (see Romans 5:3, 5).

These Christians had learned the lesson well, for other believers heard about them and the modelling spread more widely (v. 7): others learned from the Thessalonian believers what it was to be Jesus-followers, in nearby Macedonia and further-away Achaia (Corinth was that province's capital). Good models make a difference. Changed lives produce changed lives.

4 Idols then and now

What did it mean to become a Christian in first-century Thessalonica, and what does it mean today in the secularised west? The answer is remarkably similar, and this long sentence (vv. 9–10 are one sentence in Greek) lays it out: they turned, and now serve and wait.

The ancient world was full of idols which people worshipped, made from wood, stone or metal. Festivals for these idols were common, and most people would offer sacrifices in idol temples and bring their meat for the god's blessing (see 1 Corinthians 10:14–31 for how Paul helps the Corinthian Christians think this through). Jewish people were considered strange in the Greek and Roman world because they worshipped without images of the gods – for their God forbade idols (Exodus 20:4–6). Scripture mocks idols, portraying them with biting sarcasm as powerless, ineffective and no match for Israel's God (e.g. Isaiah 44:9–20). The secular west today is similar, although our idols are not statues we bow before, but the things which rule our lives and desires – classically, money, sex and power.

To become a Jesus-follower was (and is) to turn away from idols (v. 9). That the Thessalonian believers 'turned to God from idols' implies that many of them were formerly pagan, rather than Jewish. They had bowed in worship to these statues and made offerings in idol temples. But no more, for they had become God's own people. This meant that the one they served had shifted – 'serve' is used for offering sacrifice in an idol temple. Now they served the living God instead of dead, inert idols. God, known through Jesus, is active and powerful, and they experienced this in the transformation of their lives by the Holy Spirit.

Not only that, but they became Jesus-focused people (v. 10). They recognised that Jesus had liberated them from God's settled hostility against evil and idolatry in his creation, his 'wrath', which brings judgement on those who live such ways. This is clear because God raised Jesus from the dead; God-in-Christ had experienced God's wrath at the cross and overcome it, and death could not hold him. And so believers wait actively for Jesus' return from heaven, where he reigns after being raised from the dead, by living now in tune with the world-to-come which will be fully seen when Christ comes to transform this world.

5 Keeping your focus in the right place

1 Thessalonians 2:1–4

Paul, Silas and Timothy had left Thessalonica in a hurry after a mob created a disturbance there over the missionaries (Acts 17:5–10). They only had three sabbaths teaching in the synagogue (Acts 17:2) and may have stayed in the city a little longer after they became unwelcome in the synagogue. After they left, the believers would have heard criticisms of the missionary team, claiming that they had failed and that they were deceptive tricksters – Timothy may have reported this to the team (3:1–2, 6). 2:1–12 responds to such false charges, and the writers flip these claims on their head to offer positive models of Christian life and service. The latter move shifts to the real focus of the letter: to encourage and teach the believers how to walk with Christ.

The team first looks back to the visit from their perspective (1:5–10 told the story from the Thessalonians' angle). They did not see the visit as a failure (NRSV 'in vain', translating a word meaning 'empty'); rather, their time in the city was marked by courage to speak the gospel in the face of opposition (v. 2). They were hotfoot from Philippi, which they had left after a beating and an imprisonment (Acts 16:9–40), and faced vilification by unbelieving Jews in Thessalonica: verse 2 suggests that Acts 17:5 is just the tip of the iceberg of what happened. Being a gospel person in a place which rejects the gospel is tough! But the courage to speak boldly comes 'of our God' – dependence on God is vital in such situations.

Keeping the focus on God is crucial in shaping motives too. There were travelling orators who were con artists, entertaining people with clever words in order to get their money, and it is important for Paul, Silas and Timothy to distance themselves from such people. So they contrast the orators' dubious, self-centred motives (v. 3) with their approach, which focuses on God (v. 4). Christians in Sport in the UK talk about Christians playing their sport for an audience of one – in order to give God pleasure. That's what the team are interested in, for God has entrusted them with the great responsibility of being gospel communicators, and he knows their innermost thoughts and desires. That's who they look to, so they remember the privilege they have, the one they must answer to and the courage that God gives. And that's who the Thessalonians are called to look to, too.

6 Sharing our own selves

1 Thessalonians 2:5–8

Paul, Silas and Timothy continue to speak about their time in Thessalonica with the dual aims of providing the believers with answers to the criticisms others have made, and showing the believers how to live in a hostile context. They continue to draw contrasts with travelling orators to do this (as vv. 3–4). Such people came to a city to seek financial gain and praise, and perhaps to be hired by a wealthy family to exercise authority as a tutor over their children. The missionary team are different at every point.

Thus, rather than flattering people to gain their attention and their money and pretending to be other than they were (like wearing a mask, v. 5), the team kept the audience of one – God himself – in focus. They invoke God as witness to their motives, for God alone knows people's hearts and intentions. They did not seek applause from people or to be well spoken about. They didn't throw their weight around or assert their position as God's messengers (the meaning of 'apostles'). All this was anathema to them, for they were following the model of the servant Son of God himself, submitting to suffering for the sake of their divine mission.

The writers mix their metaphors by using three very different images for their gospel ministry in Thessalonica (vv. 7–8). First, they were like 'young children' (v. 7; NRSV follows different manuscripts which read 'gentle', only one letter different in Greek). They were vulnerable, not seeking power or exercising authority. Second, they were like a 'nursing mother'. As elsewhere, a feminine metaphor portrays these men's care for the believers (compare Galatians 4:19), a care like Moses' care for the people of Israel (Numbers 11:12). A mother cares intimately and dearly for her infant children as she feeds them from her own body – that was how much the team cared for the believers! Third, they were glad to share both the gospel message and their own lives with the converts, whereas travelling orators would share their message but not let people into their lives. There is no 'professional detachment' here, but the converts became 'very dear' to them (NRSV). Again, they are following the Jesus model, for he cared deeply for those near to him and even those who opposed him: he wept over Jerusalem and over Lazarus' death (Luke 19:41; John 11:35).

Guidelines

It's hard to miss the affection which the mission team of Paul, Silas and Timothy feel for the believers in Thessalonica, expressed notably by family language. As the believers heard the letter read aloud (for many could not read themselves), they would notice how often the writers call them 'brothers and sisters' – 18 times in this short letter (scan through and find them). Other groups in the ancient world used such language too, but those associations were for particular kinds of people, perhaps a trade guild, or shared ethnicity, or men of a particular status, or women (but less frequently). The early Christian assemblies were distinctive in drawing together women and men, slaves and free people, Jews and Gentiles – and their membership in a local assembly made them part of a network with other such assemblies (4:10).

As we saw in 2:5–8, the missionaries show love in their relationships with the believers. They gave themselves to the Thessalonians by imitating the model of Christ (1:6), like a nursing mother (2:7). And the believers returned this affection: they not only held the team in high regard, but loved them as family. God is their Father (1:1), and they are adopted children. So they count on each other for encouragement and support, especially when in need and when things are tough – and it certainly was tough being a Christian there and then. Paul's team fled the city because of an uprising against them (Acts 17:5, 10) and it had been a bumpy ride before that (1:6; 2:2). We shall see the writers cash out the family commitment of the believers by calling on them to care for and support each other (4:9–12, 18; 5:11, 15).

What encouragements and challenges does this feature of the letter offer to your church's relationships with each other?

1 Remember, remember, remember!

1 Thessalonians 2:9–12

Paul, Silas and Timothy continue to combat false rumours about them and to commend their lives as models of Jesus-following. They appeal to the Thessalonians' experience of them: 'you remember' (v. 9), 'you are witnesses' (v. 10) and 'you know' (v. 11) (see also vv. 1, 2, 5). The way they lived gainsaid any scandal-mongering in the city. They highlight three features of their lifestyle in this section.

First, they worked hard and long ('night and day', v. 9). Their 'toil and hard-ship' was physical work to earn a living, so that they did not need financial support. Paul was a leather-worker or tentmaker, and he practised his trade in a number of cities (e.g. Corinth, Acts 18:2–3). Indeed, his workshop gave opportunities to share the gospel with customers. His desire was to offer the gospel freely, by contrast with travelling orators, who spoke for money and favours and became 'burdens' on their supporters (see 1 Corinthians 9:18). Make the gospel freely available, including at cost to you, showing the same generosity as God – that's the message.

Second, they lived with integrity in the eyes of the Thessalonians and of God (v. 10). They lived in a way which was beyond criticism, not misleading or abusing the Thessalonians at all. Their words and manner of life were transparent, and both spoke the same message consistently. They acted justly. They did not behave well one day and badly the next. The quality of their lives, particularly their generosity and love, made an impact in Greek and Roman society driven by self-centredness and self-promotion. Live like this – that's the message.

Third, adding a further family metaphor, they acted like good fathers with their own children (vv. 11–12). Fathers were very much the 'head of the house' in this time, and some used this power to be cruel and abusive toward their children. That's not how the missionaries were: they gave encouragement, and showed and taught the believers how to live in a way which pleased God. 'Encouraging' translates a word used for compassionate care which strengthened their hands in following Christ; the Jewish author Josephus uses it for Moses calling the Israelites to be courageous in battle against a powerful foe. Not only that, but they did this one by one: 'we dealt with each of you' (v. 11). Encourage and support one another – that's the message.

2 Facing persecution

1 Thessalonians 2:13–16

The believers are having a tough time following Jesus, and they face persecu-tion for their faith. Their suffering probably included exclusion from social settings, including clubs and associations, boycotting believers' businesses, false charges against them, and verbal and physical attacks – Paul and Silas left because of a mob who attacked believers (Acts 17:5–7). The mission team encourage them in their suffering.

First, they offer a second thanksgiving, unusually in Paul's letters, echoing the first (1:2–10). Here, they focus on a particular aspect of their experience: their response to the gospel message as God's message, and not just human ideas (v. 13). They were used to travelling orators bringing human ideas to the city, but the gospel was different – it was not just passing on human ideas, but something 'at work' transforming people to be the way God intends. Take encouragement from that: the gospel message is powerful and effective.

Second, they show that persecution is normal Christian experience. The Thessalonians are not the first to suffer in this way: they follow the Judaean churches' example in suffering for their faith (v. 14). Jesus alerts his followers that they will suffer exclusion from synagogues and physical attack – even death (John 16:2–3). Even Jesus himself, as well as the scriptural prophets, experienced such hostility, so they can draw strength from him (v. 15). Take encouragement from that: you're not alone and follow your Lord in suffering.

Third, they encourage the believers that present persecution is not the last word. The time will come when those who attack and hurt them must answer to God, for God loves his people and is deeply committed to them (v. 16). In facing suffering, they are to take encouragement that God will act justly in their defence.

It would be easy to misread verses 14–16 as an attack on the Jewish people as a whole, and a naughty comma in NRSV at the end of verse 14 encourages that. NRSV's comma (absent in the Greek) suggests that 'the Jews' as a whole are responsible for the terrible deeds of verses 15–16. The awful history of antisemitism in the churches is the legacy of misreading in this way. NIV rightly omits the comma: the Jews who displease God are those who killed the Lord Jesus and the prophets, *not* all Jews – Paul himself is Jewish, after all, and is passionately concerned for Jewish people to become believers (e.g. Romans 9:1–3).

3 Absence and desire

1 Thessalonians 2:17–20

Paul, Silas and Timothy reminded the believers of their conduct when they were in Thessalonica earlier (2:1–12), and now turn to what has happened since they left the city. It's possible that there was concern among the believers that the team had abandoned them, or criticism by outsiders that the missionaries couldn't care much, if they didn't return.

The missionaries fled from Thessalonica to Beroea (Acts 17:10), and that's probably what's meant by being 'orphaned' from you (v. 17). They felt like orphaned children: vulnerable and in pain at the separation. It's a family word again – see 'Remember, remember, remember', above. They underline their concern by their eager longing to see the believers again (vv. 17–18). Paul himself injects a personal note to say how much he personally wanted to return (v. 18) – maybe Paul, as the team leader, was being particularly criticised over his absence. The lack of visit was not because of lack of desire to visit.

The team made repeated attempts to return, but at the bottom of their failure was Satan's work (v. 18). Paul writes of his 'thorn in the flesh' as Satan's messenger (2 Corinthians 12:7–8), most probably referring to either physical illness or persecution, and something similar may be in view here. They are writing from Corinth after running from Thessalonica to Beroea to Athens because of persecution. Paul is far from interpreting the slightest problem as Satan at work, but he is also not naive about the reality of personal evil opposing the spread of the gospel and the building-up of churches.

The writers emphasise their love and commitment to the Christians using a series of images (vv. 19–20). The believers fill them with hope that God will complete the work he has begun in them, and joy at their progress. As parents take delight in their children, so the team with the Thessalonians: they are their 'crown of boasting' (NRSV), an image from athletic competitions in which the winner was crowned with a laurel wreath to honour their victory (see also 1 Corinthians 9:25). Taking pride in those you help come to faith and grow in faith is appropriate and, the team imply, will lead to God rewarding them when Christ returns (v. 19).

4 Paul's pastoral passion

1 Thessalonians 3:1–8

We heard Paul's pastoral passion earlier, as he looks back to the initial visit to Thessalonica (2:1–12) and expresses his concern for them when away (2:17–20). Paul now reveals the depth of his love for the believers. Lack of information was causing Paul to worry that everything the mission team did might have come to nothing, particularly because he knew the spiritual opposition they faced from Satan, 'the tempter' (v. 5). So finally Paul sent Timothy from Athens (vv. 1–2), where he had fled after being rejected in

Beroea (Acts 17:13–15). Paul missed Timothy's companionship and support in gospel ministry, but he knew that Timothy was well equipped to encourage the believers in a tough situation (v. 2).

Paul was not guessing that the Thessalonian believers were suffering for their faith: he knew that persecution is normal Christian living and had taught them that during his initial visit (v. 4; see also 2:14–16). God is not a sadist, wanting his people to suffer because it pleases him; rather, as believers swim against the tide of the world's way of living and thinking, they inevitably face the currents of opposition. In this they follow the model of Jesus himself, who walked the path of suffering to the cross in humble service of his Father and the human race (see 2:14–15). For Christians in the west today, persecution can be more subtle than physical and verbal assaults. Nevertheless, Paul's warning is vital, for we, too, follow in the steps of a suffering saviour, and live in societies shaped by unbelieving worldviews, under the influence of evil powers.

Paul's relief on hearing good news from Timothy is palpable (vv. 6–8)! Paul is not a lone-ranger Christian unaffected by others: his heart beats in time with God's heart, longing for the believers to stand firm and grow in their faith. Paul rejoices in the news of their 'faith and love' (v. 6). Here, 'faithfulness' may be a better translation, for it is their continuing loyalty to Christ which is in view. Their 'love' is multi-dimensional: for the Lord in whom they stand firm (v. 8); for the mission team, whom they remember with joy, and long to see, perhaps particularly Paul (v. 6); and Paul probably has their love for one another in mind too, for he wanted them to copy the team's model of selfless love (2:11–12; 3:12). Paul is now truly alive because of their faithfulness to the Lord (v. 8)!

5 Thanks and requests

1 Thessalonians 3:9–13

The good news from Timothy (v. 6) leads naturally to prayer. First, the team give God thanks for the believers (v. 9). Their thanks are 'in return for' the team's joy: the way to respond to good things coming from God is to say 'Thank you' – as I was taught to write thank-you letters to relatives who sent birthday and Christmas gifts. A rejoicing heart should be a thankful heart.

Next, the team intercede, first telling the believers what they pray – that they will visit Thessalonica again (v. 10) – and then addressing God and the

Lord Jesus directly to ask for that and other things (vv. 11–13). On a few occasions, I have written to friends to say what I'm praying for them, and they've told me how encouraging it is to know that. What do Paul, Silas and Timothy ask?

First, notice that they pray to God the Father and the Lord Jesus (v. 11); in this early letter, it's clear that it is appropriate to pray to Jesus alongside the Father. The team assume the Lord Jesus has power to act in this world and to make the path straight to them (v. 11, 'clear the way'; other translations have 'direct our way'). A straight road is the shortest distance between two places, and that's the image: they want to be back in Thessalonica as soon as possible, and they ask God to make that happen.

Second, they pray for growing love among the believers which spills over to outsiders (v. 12). Paul, Silas and Timothy aren't thinking that they don't love (see 4:9–10); rather, they ask for increasing love. A key attraction for people to Christianity, in the ancient world and today, is genuine, wholehearted love. For the Thessalonians, as for other early believers, this might mean providing for people in poverty or caring for those who were ill. This is something to pray for today!

Third, they pray for stronger hearts. We think of the heart as the seat of emotions, but in the ancient world, it was the place of the will and decision-making. The team pray that the choices the believers make will be godly, so that when they see Christ face-to-face at the last day, they will be without fault, reflecting God's own holiness. There will be more to say about the last day later (4:13—5:11), but for now the team pray for (as we might say) wise decisions and wills directed to please God.

6 Pleasing God more and more

1 Thessalonians 4:1–8

The missionaries remind the believers of the call to holiness (v. 7, and the word behind sanctification, v. 3) – living differently as people who belong to Christ, rather than going with the flow of society around them. Their top priority is 'to please God' (v. 1), and how that audience of one sees things is to be their concern. Paul, Timothy and Silas make clear that they know that the Thessalonians are living this way (v. 1), which was the good news Timothy brought (3:6).

They then zero in on sexual conduct as a key area of holy living. It's not that they are obsessed with sex, as some today accuse Christians of being; rather, they are very aware of the sexual standards of their culture and time and recognise that those standards are out of line with God's purposes. Men – especially rich and powerful men – were at liberty to have sex with different women with impunity, including prostitutes. The philosopher Demosthenes wrote, 'We keep mistresses for pleasure, concubines for our day-to-day bodily needs, but we have wives to produce legitimate children and serve as trustworthy guardians of our homes.' So one danger the missionaries warn against is having sex with another man's wife, 'wrong[ing] or [taking] advantage of a brother or sister' (v. 6) – that would be destructive of marriage and the trust believers should have in one another as God's family.

The writers are seeking to avoid believers getting into situations where they can easily succumb to sexual temptation: we could translate 'distance yourselves from sexual immorality' (v. 3). This means staying as far away as possible from it – not going as near as possible without actually committing sin. The instruction is like saying they should drive in the middle of the road, to avoid sliding into the gutter. Because humans are embodied creatures, it's about controlling our bodies, rather than giving in to whatever our appetites desire (vv. 4–5). Our bodies are gifts from God, redeemed by Christ, and what we do with our bodies matters to God.

Joseph is a great example of this at work (Genesis 39:1–12). His master's wife persistently asked him to have sex with her, and Joseph's response was to say that he would not do that to Potiphar or 'sin against God' (v. 9) – and he ran away. He lived his life under God's eye, and pleasing God in what he did with his body was part of that.

Guidelines

Paul, Silas and Timothy recognise the pressure the Thessalonian believers face, including outright persecution (2:13–15; 3:2–5) and sexual immorality (4:3–8). Paul himself was distressed that he could not visit to encourage them, so he sent Timothy (3:1–2) and the team then wrote this letter (3:6). They offer three resources for holy living in an unholy world – it's worth reflecting on how we draw on these in following Jesus today.

First and foremost, the believers are motivated by knowing that they live before God, and their greatest desire is to please God (2:4; 4:1). This is akin to Hebrews' call to keep our eyes fixed on Jesus (Hebrews 12:1–2). It's easy to lose focus on God amid the day's activities, and it's worth finding ways to remind ourselves to refocus on Christ as the day goes on – such as by a key phrase or picture stuck to our mirror, or in a pocket or handbag, or somewhere we work.

Second, these Christians have the 'help of our God', as the missionary team did (2:2). This includes, of course, remembering the gospel message they brought (2:2, 4, 8, 9, 13). It also includes prayer for each other: the missionaries encourage the Thessalonians that they are praying for them (3:10), implicitly calling them to do the same for each other. They aren't called to walk the Christian road alone, but God's power is available to them by the Spirit (1:5).

Third, these Christians have sisters and brothers in faith for encouragement, in the city and more widely, including their memory of the team's visit and their love for the believers (2:1–12), and the encouragement of others who stand for Christ amidst suffering (2:14–16). They belong to a worldwide and local community of believers – they are not alone.

1   Let's go to Philadelphia!

1 Thessalonians 4:9–12

'Love of the brothers and sisters' (v. 9 NRSV) is the Greek word philadelphia, which gave an American city its name. Prior to early Christianity, it appears less than a dozen times in Greek literature, but it became a key word for how Christians were to treat one another. It's one of a number of examples of 'family' language used for the believing communities in this letter (see 1:4; 2:1, 7, 9, 11, 17; 3:7, 11; 4:1, 10). As believers are God's children through Jesus, they are therefore each other's sisters and brothers and should relate to each other as family. Paul, Silas and Timothy are delighted that this is how the Thessalonians live, including caring for believers in other cities in the province of Macedonia (vv. 9–10). They learned this love from God, imparted by the Spirit (v. 9; note v. 8). As with holy living, the team urge the believers to do this 'more and more' (v. 10; compare v. 1).

Why do they then talk about daily life and work (vv. 11–12)? Most probably it is because love is not an abstract idea, but is seen in everyday life. Most people in the ancient Roman world were part of the web of patron-client relationship which flowed out from the emperor, the ultimate patron. Patrons provided food or resources for their clients, and clients in return supported their patrons, such as by going to hear their patron speak in the city senate and applauding them – the relationship was governed by reciprocal commitment. Clients were dependent financially on their patrons, and so could not act or speak in ways the patron did not like or agree with.

The missionaries want Christians not to be in such dependent relationships with patrons, but to be free to live out their faith in daily life – for if their patron was not a believer, that would be incredibly difficult. This is what the writers mean by saying the believers should lead a 'quiet life' and 'mind your own affairs' (v. 11). They are to avoid the competitiveness of Greek and Roman society and work independently, including physical labour 'with your hands' (v. 11), as the missionaries had (2:9). Such behaviour will show outsiders that they are dependable and honest people, not beholden to or dependent on a patron. It will also mean that they can support people in need, especially fellow Christians (compare 'help the weak', 5:14).

2 The dead in Christ

1 Thessalonians 4:13–18

The letter-senders now respond to an issue which seems to be a particular concern of the Thessalonian believers: the fate of believers who die before the return of Jesus. Jesus' coming again was part of their initial gospel proclamation in the city (1:10), but the missionaries had had to leave the city after a relatively brief time. That meant they could not teach as fully as in cities where they stayed longer, such as Corinth (Acts 18:11) or Ephesus (Acts 19:10). It looks as if the death of believers had led to questions about what would happen to them at the Lord's return; it may be that some believers were actually killed for their faith, which would raise the question even more acutely.

Paul, Silas and Timothy do not encourage denying the grief that the death of loved ones brings, but they do encourage a grief different from that of non-believers (v. 13). Christian grief acknowledges the pain of separation and loss, but also recognises the hope that Christ brings of life in the world to come. Hope mitigates grief, but does not wipe it away.

The missionaries use the image of 'sleep' for death (vv. 13–15, using the metaphor 'fall asleep/sleep in death'; NRSV hides the metaphor by translating 'who have died'). This was an image of death used in the ancient world, but in Christianity it was transformed by the resurrection of Jesus. No longer would dead people sleep permanently in death, but believers could look forward to the day of Christ's return when they will be raised – and the dead will take prime place on that day (vv. 15–16).

Verses 16–17 have given rise to mistaken speculation about a 'rapture' of Christians flying up into the heavens and disappearing from the earth. But the image of meeting the Lord in the air uses a Greek word commonly used for the official visit of a dignitary to a city. The city elders would go about half a mile out of the city to meet the dignitary, and would then accompany them into the city. Here, Jesus is 'the Lord', the supreme dignitary, and this image suggests that he will meet living believers accompanied by those who died, and they will then travel *to earth*, an earth which Jesus will transform and renew (see Revelation 21). It is there – on this renewed earth – that 'we will be with the Lord forever' (v. 17). Some encouragement (v. 18)!

3 Coming like a thief

1 Thessalonians 5:1–5

The writers' focus continues to be on the Lord's return, but it now shifts from Christians who have died (4:13–18) to those who now live (5:1–11). There was evidently debate about when events would take place in relation to the Lord's return, 'times and dates' (v. 1). Paul, Silas and Timothy remind the believers that they know that day is unpredictable – like a thief's coming (v. 2). Thieves don't send a text message to let a householder know when they will break in; the element of surprise is essential to their success! Jesus uses this image about coming events (e.g. Matthew 24:43), and the image recurs in Revelation (3:3; 16:15).

Some were saying that all would be well, using the slogan 'peace and safety' (v. 3). It's unclear exactly who these people were and what their agenda was, but the missionaries are clear that such people will be taken by surprise when the judgement of the day of the Lord comes upon them. They use a feminine image, of a pregnant woman experiencing labour pains, to illustrate the point. A pregnant woman knows the time will come when she has labour pains, and that will be the prelude (all being well) to the arrival of her child. These pains are inevitable, but unpredictable. That's why many pregnant women keep a bag packed with the things they will need in hospital when they give birth, ready to go.

Likewise, since Jesus' coming can be at any time, the practical implication is being alert and awake, ready for that day. The missionaries use images of day and night to convey the importance of acting like 'children of the day' (vv. 4–5). The Old Testament is full of images of light and darkness: light is about living in wisdom (Ecclesiastes 2:13), experiencing God's salvation (Psalm 18:28) and living God's way in response to his teaching (Psalm 119:105, 130). That's what the missionaries call the Thessalonians to do: to walk faithfully with God by the Spirit's power. They will say more about what 'being ready' looks like in the next section (vv. 6–11).

4 Light and lifestyle

1 Thessalonians 5:6–11

With 'so then' (v. 6), the writers transition to spelling out the implications of the unpredictable date of the Lord's return. Knowing and believing in Jesus' return is something which should earth Christians into living for Christ today, rather than speculating about the future, and our authors now show how this looks. The section's development is signalled by a series of connecting words: the writers make a statement (v. 6, 'So then'), explain it (v. 7, 'For'), draw a contrast to underline the first statement (v. 8, 'But'), and then support this point (vv. 9–10 'For'), before drawing a conclusion (v. 11, 'Therefore'). Read over the section two or three times to see how this development works.

Christian lifestyle in this dark, night-filled world is to be like a beam of sunshine into a dark place. The believers' lives are to be characterised by vigilance (v. 6), like the five bridesmaids who had enough oil to keep their lamps burning when the bridegroom arrived (Matthew 25:1–13). By contrast with the people of darkness around them, the Thessalonians are to take on God's own armour of loyalty/faith, love and hope (v. 8, echoing 1:3). The writers develop an idea from scripture here, for the armour was originally God's armour, worn to fight on behalf of his people (Isaiah 59:17). Now it becomes God's people's armour, enabling them to stand firm amid a hostile society. Fidelity to Christ and love for him and his people are the breastplate which protects the vital organs from penetration by enemy weapons; staying close to Jesus and loving their brothers and sisters are vital to their safety. The helmet, protecting the head, is the hope consisting of salvation, looking forward with confidence in God's promises and character to the day of the Lord when believers will be vindicated.

Christian confidence in our salvation is not arrogance, as some say. If salvation depended on us and the quality of our faith, love and hope, we would all be lost. But the truth is that it depends on God, whose purpose for believers is salvation, a salvation accomplished by Jesus in his death. That's where Christian confidence lies – in what God has done in Christ. The writers call on the Thessalonians to keep their focus there, for that's why they live – in trusting in him (v. 10). That's worth sharing with others (v. 11)!

5 Living in peace

1 Thessalonians 5:12–15

Yes, criticism of church leaders seems to go back to the very beginning (vv. 12–13)! Paul, Silas and Timothy urge the believers to 'hold them in the highest regard in love because of their work' (v. 13). They are writing, remember, in response to Timothy's news of what's happening in Thessalonica (3:6), and so are probably addressing an issue or a potential issue there. It may be that the pressure from outsiders which we've noticed throughout the letter was causing stresses in relationships within the church – external criticism and persecution certainly have the danger of dividing Christians. You don't have to agree with everything a leader says to hold them in high regard – and notice that the missionaries urge respect rather than obedience to leaders. They are under no illusion that leaders always get it right, but they do recognise the vital importance of support and encouragement for leaders.

Rather than be divided and mutually distrustful, the writers urge the believers to 'live in peace with each other' (v. 13). This is an ethic of treating others with respect and high regard as sisters and brothers in Christ, and it's developed in the rest of this section in six calls to action, a mixture of ways to act and not to act; read through verses 14–15 and identify them.

Each of these six calls unpacks what it means to 'live in peace' (v. 13). They include speaking positively to support others and negatively to warn people who are freeloaders, relying on other believers' generosity or their patrons' provision (see 4:9–12). The encouragement, help and patience of other Christians are critical when life is tough, whether through physical illness, discouragement or serious personal or financial problems.

Similarly, when you think someone has wronged you, it's easy to respond in kind, to pay them back for what they did. The missionaries call for a refusal to act that way, because they know that this is how God has treated believers through Jesus Christ. On the cross, Jesus took upon himself human sin and hatred, and neutralised it. His resurrection was God's vindication of his death, showing that the powers of evil were defeated. His people are called to live that out by acting as Christ did, aiming to do good to everyone (v. 15). They challenge their readers to act toward others as God acts toward them – that's quite a challenge!

6 Final words

1 Thessalonians 5:16–28

Paul's letters regularly end with a series of crisp exhortations which draw together key points of the letter. They aren't just generic Christian-speak, but address the readers directly. Here (vv. 16–22), the missionary team refocus their readers on what God wants for them (v. 18). In the context of believers dying (see 4:13–18), some of the Thessalonians could be wondering if they had misunderstood what God wants, and so Paul, Silas and Timothy help them see how to find God's purpose for them in this situation.

Giving thanks 'in all circumstances' is not the same as giving thanks *for* all circumstances (v. 18). The missionaries call their friends to be thankful, praying people whatever their circumstances. Thanksgiving is about recognising the good things God has done and given to us and expressing that verbally; it's all too easy to forget this. The old song 'Count your blessings, name them one by one' highlights an important truth – we cannot outgive God, who has given us all things in Jesus Christ, and we owe God thanks for these things.

A further key thing in knowing God's will is right listening to the Spirit, who speaks through prophetic words to a community (vv. 19–20). Perhaps some in the community were over-cautious about prophecy, or over-gullible to anything said in the Lord's name. In either case, the right response is testing, seeking to know if this is truly God's word to the community (v. 21). That testing would involve whether the words lined up with who God is according to scripture and God's work in and through Jesus.

Finally, the team pray for the Thessalonians (vv. 23–24) and send greetings (vv. 25–27). As earlier, they share the content of their prayer with the recipients (e.g. 3:10–13), to encourage them – an encouragement which will grow as God answers those prayers. They pray for holiness of life, a key theme of the letter (see 3:13; 4:3–4, 7), a holiness which pervades every aspect of their lives, 'spirit, soul and body'.

The writers express great warmth and affection for the believers in these closing words, again addressing them as 'brothers and sisters' (v. 25) and seeking their prayers – the praying relationship is two-way. They want nothing more than God's generous love in the Lord Jesus Christ to be present to strengthen and uphold them in their walk with God (v. 28).

Guidelines

I was once a bishop's chaplain, and one of my duties was filtering the bishop's mail. Some letters needed a careful and wise answer, particularly those complaining about a vicar. There was a steady trickle of such letters, and they involved research and a careful response. Sometimes the letter-writer had not even spoken to the minister about the issue. Sadly, I cannot recall the bishop ever getting a letter saying how pleased church members were with their vicar, or thanking the bishop for appointing a wise and godly man or woman to their church. People only ever wrote to complain!

Christian leaders are rightly held to a high standard, and this letter speaks of the missionaries' own example (2:1–12). Where leaders act improperly – as has happened very publicly over the years and in recent times – there needs to be appropriate accountability and answerability.

That said, our letter's call to honour hard-working church leaders (5:12–13) is striking in the light of the bishop's postbag. Church leaders have to assess when people need warmth and support and when they need to be admonished – set back on the right path from which they've deviated. This is difficult, particularly when the minister is appointed entirely by the local church, and may fear losing their job if they say the wrong thing or challenge powerful church people.

If a local church is known for its internal fighting, that is incredibly unattractive to their community and damages gospel witness in the area for years to come. This letter invites and challenges us to be encouragers of our leaders, not by gullibly accepting everything they do as being God's will, but by speaking and acting in ways that will build them up, not tear them down. How can you do that?

FURTHER READING

Nijay K. Gupta, *1–2 Thessalonians* (New Covenant Commentary Series) (Cascade, 2016) – If you'd like to dig deeper into this letter, this short commentary provides helpful reflections on the letter's implications for today. You'll also find it helpful when we study 2 Thessalonians in a few months' time.

Middle age

Russell Herbert

A precise definition of midlife is tricky. None of us know when we're midway through life because we don't know how long we will live! Life expectancy is longer today than for previous generations, so middle age might now be regarded as something that begins later. For all such ambiguity, there is a season of our lives in which we are neither young nor old. That's middle age.

Much has been written about the 'midlife crisis'. The origin of the term has been attributed to psychoanalyst Elliot Jacques, who in 1965 published a study of perceived changes in creativity among artists entering their mid-30s. Jacques documented a process of coming to terms with being on a declining path leading to death. Prior to this, Carl Jung (1875–1961) described how, at some point between 35 and 40 years, the developmental focus shifts away from establishing ourselves in society, towards a process of *individuation*. This involves the pursuit of meaning and understanding who we really are. Jung said it is no use trying to live the second half of life as though it were the same as the first.

Whether or not we would regard our experience of midlife as a 'crisis', humans are essentially searching, questioning beings. On entering middle age, we can find ourselves both looking back and gazing forward with a deep sense of challenge. We may feel that time is running out. Yet we have the vantage point of learned experience which we did not have the benefit of in our youth.

I hope that the Bible passages that follow will help us to consider some of the issues that we might wrestle with, particularly in middle age. The eternal perspective of Christian hope offers a transformative way of understanding.

Unless otherwise stated, Bible quotations are taken from the NRSV.

1 Learning to be content

Philippians 4

Philippians 4 is all about exhortation and encouragement, not a reflection on the experience of entering middle age. Yet Paul's words speak powerfully into what can be one of the most hounding midlife questions: 'What have I achieved?' We might bemoan how we have fallen short of the aspirations of our youth, and looking forward it can feel as if there is little time left to fulfil those hopes and dreams.

The vantage point of midlife might afford us some learned wisdom, such as mistakes to avoid in the years ahead. But Paul offers something far more precious. He shares how his attitude towards changing circumstances has been shaped and formed. He has 'learned to be content'. The word 'content' (v. 11) is from the Greek αὐτάρκης. It denotes a state of being 'sufficient', independent of external circumstances. Within Stoic thinking, this would mean complete 'self-sufficiency', the virtue of being emotionally untouched by anything going on around us. But for Paul, the meaning is 'God-sufficiency'. Here, the depth of satisfaction through relationship with God surpasses the positivity and negativity of ever-shifting circumstance. It is a gift of God's grace, but Paul says it is something he has had to *learn*. It seems this may not have come easily and that he had to work on it over time with effort and discipline. Thus, we should be neither surprised nor discouraged if we find the call to cultivate contentment challenging.

It could easily be assumed that Paul's main concern is contentment in the face of hardship. But he speaks of learning to be content while being 'well-fed' and 'having plenty' (v. 12). One of the greatest challenges can be breaking cycles of dissatisfaction. Achievement has this awful habit of blinding us to the realities for which we should be thankful. Hence, Paul urges us to rejoice 'always' (v. 4) and to make our requests to God 'with thanksgiving' (v. 6). Middle age gives us the opportunity to discern and celebrate the blessings of life's achievements so far. Paul's exhortation to rejoice 'in the Lord' (v. 4) reminds us that fulfilment is not to be found in those finite blessings, but in God, who is eternal.

2 Work in progress

The Bible might not specifically address middle age, but it does present a vision of growth and maturity.

Not long after my 36th birthday, it occurred to me that 18 years had passed since becoming 18. 'Adulthood come of age', perhaps? More than a decade has passed since then, and although I might like to think of myself as spiritually mature, the truth is that I know I've still got a lot of growing up to do.

In middle age, we can look back at our youth and recall the sort of people we hoped we might become. The contrast of those aspirations with the reality we find decades later can be unsettling. We might take a look at ourselves now and cringe at how far we fall short of those ideals.

Paul's vision of maturity is grand (vv. 12–17), yet it is realistic and full of hope. We are to see ourselves as work in progress. Paul doesn't say this out of a sense of resignation to our shortcomings, but with confidence that from God's eternal perspective, we can see our lives as a journey, on our way to greater things (vv. 1–4).

Our identity is in Christ, in whom we have resurrection (v. 1). Because Christian hope looks to resurrection and the promised kingdom of God, which will come in fullness at the end of time, there's a sense in which we can interpret our imperfection as caught up in that tension between the 'already' and the 'not yet'. God's kingdom is coming, but it's still ahead of us in the future. Paul writes, 'Your life is hidden with Christ in God' (v. 3). Therefore we can understand our identity as something that is on the road to being made whole. It gives us a meaningful way of recognising that while we may be broken, we need not cringe or despair. Things will not always be like this. In Christ we are saved, but the best is yet to come.

3 Net worth

Enter the name of any celebrity on Google and notice the search prediction complete the sentence with 'net worth'. By the time we reach middle age, we are likely to have been immersed for years in a culture that perceives success primarily in terms of wealth.

Money itself is morally and spiritually neutral – it is neither good nor bad. However, there is no neutrality when it comes to our *relationship* with money. Jesus appears to have devoted a lot of time warning about the dangers of attachment to it. It is not difficult to understand why.

Money is arguably the obvious alternative to the things that God promises. God and money have a lot in common; both offer provision, peace of mind, security and satisfaction. The list could go on. Money is God's biggest rival because it is the one thing that we are most likely to be attracted towards when searching for something tangible in which to place our trust and confidence. Little wonder Jesus says we must choose one or the other (v. 24).

Midlife can be a time when reflection on personal identity intensifies. In a society that persistently measures value in financial terms, the question of personal worth confronts us, forcing us to ask how far we have 'climbed the ladder', whether that refers to career or property, and how far might we increase our power to earn and spend in our remaining time.

Throughout Matthew 6, Jesus' teaching brings us back to a fundamental challenge: do we serve God or money? Our response will shape our identity. The heart is where the treasure is (v. 21). Financial giving, fasting and self-denial are perhaps the most intimate expressions of our relationship with God (vv. 1–4, 16–18). Living in hopeful expectation of the everlasting kingdom (v. 10) involves trusting that God will meet our daily needs (v. 11). Setting our hearts on the pursuit of wealth is a dangerous distraction from the extraordinary riches that await in eternity (vv. 19–20). Looking at the world and valuing it through the lens of eternity enables us to walk in the light (v. 22), whereas preoccupation with unhealthy interests brings only darkness and destruction (v. 23). But we are not to worry (vv. 25–34). God has sustained us this far in life, and always will.

4 Compassion fatigue

Galatians 6

I once saw a T-shirt bearing the message, 'I'm not cynical, just experienced.' Life experience can breed scepticism. There is a danger that upon entering middle age we have unwittingly embraced suspicion as a virtue, regarding it more highly than what we have perhaps come to consider as the naivete of our younger years.

Sustaining care and compassion towards others requires effort. In Galatians 6, Paul makes an appeal. It seems he is all too aware that patience can be strained by relationships (v. 17). Tempting though it may be to give up, we must not grow weary (v. 9). Paul's exhortation is not targeted towards people in midlife or any other specific age group. Yet his words of warning have heightened significance when we reflect on the learned cynicism that can all too easily surface in middle age. Simply put, if we are to genuinely fulfil what is required of us as disciples of Jesus, we are to readily bear one another's burdens (v. 2).

Paul knows that people can be difficult, and he makes it clear that certain behaviours need to be confronted. But our attitude to addressing the shortcomings of others is never to be one of judgementalism. Rather, our aim is to be that of restoration, always by way of gentleness (v. 1). In the same verse, Paul highlights that this is a feature of the presence of the Spirit, and there are echoes of the preceding chapter (5:22–23), where gentleness is named in his description of the fruit of the Spirit.

A hallmark of Spirit-filled gentleness is humility. Paul points out that when there is tough talking to be done in seeking to restore others, personal pride only ever gets in the way (v. 3). Learned cynicism blinds us to our own weakness. We should beware such self-deception (v. 7). We are all accountable before the one in whose grace we are sustained (v. 5).

Should we find our compassion towards others eroding, we may need to rediscover the important spiritual principle that we reap what we sow (vv. 7–8). We should regard the needs of others as 'opportunities' to do good (v. 10).

Paul's reference to circumcision (vv. 12–15) reminds us of the perils of religious legalism. Middle-aged Christians are often longstanding believers, and we should strive to ensure that our attitude to others is shaped by nothing other than the grace of Jesus (v. 18).

5 If only…

Middle age can be dogged by the voice of 'if only'. This can take the form of a sense of missed opportunity; a hunch that things could have been better; an ache to go back and reset a particular course of action. But then there is a more haunting type of regret – the kind that has to do with guilt. This is more complex because it involves relationships and damage to others. This has a greater tendency to linger. Shame clings.

In Philippians 3, Paul bids us to break from any preoccupation with the past. His starting point is that of challenging the religious legalism from which Christ sets us free (vv. 2–6). Christ changes everything. Knowing him is the one and only thing that matters now, because it is in that relationship that we encounter the power of the resurrection (vv. 7–11). This eternal perspective transforms the way we are to look at the past, and so walk in the present.

Paul urges us to look forward, not back (v. 12). All forms of regret focus on the past. Whatever may be going on in our lives in middle age, listening to the voice of 'if only' drags us back. Like being tethered with a piece of strong elastic, every time we attempt to move forward, regret causes resistance. Effort is required, hence Paul's insistence that we must 'press on' (vv. 12, 14), 'straining forward to what lies ahead' (v. 13).

Living with our faces set towards the future raises the existential question of how we might find a meaningful way of being in the present moment. But authentic biblical hope does not empty the significance of the here and now, or deny us the ability to simply 'be' in the moment. Paul helps us understand how, by reminding us that 'our citizenship is in heaven' (v. 20). Faith is not a ticket to eternity, but there is a sense in which it functions a bit like a passport, reminding us of our identity in Christ who promises future resurrection. Such hope empowers us to embrace the present and go forth in it, transformed by future expectation and released from the grip of the past (vv. 20–21).

6 Embracing the second half

2 Corinthians 4

Given that we do not know how long we will live, it might be presumptuous to refer to the rest of our lives as the 'second half'. However long remains, looking beyond middle age can be sobering. We may be struck by the possibility that we have lived more years already than are left ahead. Time seems to pass with increasing speed. Our bodies start to remind us that we are not getting any younger. The motivating power of visionary ambition can sap away. It can be difficult to frame a sense of future with the same anticipatory zest we once knew.

The eternal perspective of Christian hope challenges any 'downhill from here' mindset. In 2 Corinthians 4, Paul insists, 'We do not lose heart' (v. 1). He begins that sentence with 'therefore' – a word that points back to the preceding chapter, where Paul describes the transforming power of the Spirit which enables us to see 'the glory of the Lord' (3:16–18). It is this vision of Christ that is set before us. Our faces are unveiled, and as such our outlook should not be bleak, but bright. The darkness is flooded with the light of Christ (vv. 3–6).

Paul is utterly realistic, though. We have 'treasure in clay jars' (v. 7). Our bodies are fragile, and we may face the realities of being afflicted, perplexed, persecuted and struck down; yet God's power in us means we are not crushed, driven to despair, forsaken or destroyed (vv. 8–9). We carry the death of Jesus in our bodies, but precisely because of this, we also carry his life (vv. 10–11). Yes, there is a real sense in which we are 'wasting away' as we age. But inner renewal becomes deeper, stronger and ever-more powerful. Thus Paul reiterates, 'We do not lose heart' (v. 16).

Middle age confronts us with the truth that life is short. We are in the process of dying. Paul refers to 'this slight momentary affliction' because he sees it in eternal perspective (vv. 17–18). The best is yet to come. It will last forever. Until then, there's living to be done. This involves ageing and dying, but it doesn't end there.

Guidelines

When Peter addressed the crowd at Pentecost, he quoted the prophet Joel, 'your young men shall see visions, and your old men shall dream dreams' (Acts 2:17). Nothing was said about middle age! The proposition that midlife is the harbinger of an existential crisis is a much more recent phenomenon. Nevertheless, scripture has much to say about issues we might wrestle with through these middle years. The eternal perspective of Christian hope enables us to see things through a different lens.

- To what extent does your understanding of God shape your idea of what it means to be content?
- How might understanding life as a process of growth enable the letting go of the past?
- In looking back on your life so far, what is your 'if only…'? If you were to ask God to help you turn that into a 'what if…', what might it look like?
- How might contemplating eternity shape our approach to the future?

FURTHER READING

Bob Buford, *Half Time* (Zondervan, 2008).

Russell Herbert, *Halfway Home? Finding faith in midlife* (Kevin Mayhew, 2019).

Tony Horsfall, *Spiritual Growth in a Time of Change: Following God in midlife* (BRF, 2016).

Nick Page, *The Dark Night of the Shed: Men, the midlife crisis, spirituality and sheds* (Hodder and Stoughton, 2015).

Paul Robb, *Passage through Midlife: A spiritual journey to wholeness* (Ave Maria Press, 2005).

Richard Rohr, *Falling Upward* (SPCK, 2011).

Paul David Tripp, *Lost in the Middle: Midlife and the grace of God* (Shepherd Press, 2004).

Pentecost

Freddy Hedley

The manifestation of the Holy Spirit at Pentecost in Acts 2 marks a pivotal point in the biblical narrative, on the journey from creation to new creation. On the one hand it ushers in a new era for the people of God with the inauguration of the church. On the other, it represents the culmination of God's desire and plan to live among and within his people. It is this second aspect that we will focus on throughout this week.

We will begin at the beginning, by reflecting on the blueprint of God's plan revealed in Genesis 1, noting particularly God's intention for humanity to share the blessing of his presence. Tragically, this relationship was fractured in the aftermath of Eden, resulting in the separation of humanity from God's presence, but the relationship was not beyond repair. Thus, we will proceed to trace the biblical story through the week by focusing on some of the key passages which unveil God's response to humanity's separation from his presence. We will reflect on Israel's encounter with God in Exodus 19, the establishment of the Jerusalem temple as God's house in 2 Chronicles 7 and the prophetic promises of God's restored Spirit and glory among his people in Zechariah 2 and Haggai 2, before turning, finally, to the full restoration of God's presence dwelling within his people with the gift of the Holy Spirit at Pentecost in Acts 2.

By tracing this story, my hope is that as we come to celebrate Pentecost, we do so with a renewed appreciation for the momentous completion it represented, as well as the vital new ground that was broken, which continues to bless the church to this day.

Unless otherwise stated, Bible quotations are taken from the NRSV.

1   The first foundations

Genesis 1:1–28

The Bible opens with a wondrous introduction to the creator of all things. Over the years, the importance and meaning of this passage has been regularly debated, both inside and outside the church. So often, the focus is on two questions: how was the world created and when did it happen? These questions come from the deepest of human needs, to understand our place in creation. However, when read in context, it becomes clear that Genesis 1 has been crafted to meet this need by answering different questions: not how and when, but who and why. There is nothing about the physical description of the earth or the process of its origin that would have greatly stood out from the cosmology of Israel's ancient Near Eastern neighbours. Where Genesis 1 differs radically, however, is in its understanding of who God and humanity are.

Contrary to every surrounding nation, Israel's primary creation story proclaims *one God*, not many. The Hebrew word for 'God' used throughout this passage (*elohim*) does in fact resemble a Hebrew masculine plural noun, but all of the corresponding verbs are singular and thus so is *elohim*. Moreover, he is sovereign over all creation, works in relational partnership with those he creates (note, for example, how the land, not God, creates the plants in vv. 11–12) and is the source of all good – far from the tyrannical localised deities worshipped by Israel's neighbours.

Those neighbours also held a low view of humanity. In Mesopotamia, humanity was made to be a slave of the gods. In one Egyptian myth, humanity was the accidental by-product of the god of creation's tears. Genesis 1, however, declares humanity to be the image of God (vv. 26–27) – a title commonly reserved for kings across the ancient world. A second significant resonance of the word for 'image' (*tselem*) is with temple idols (e.g. 2 Kings 11:18; Ezekiel 16:17; Amos 5:26). In ancient times, idols were believed to be objects that, once formed into the likeness of a god, would contain the physical presence of that god. Such an association has massive implications for the readers of Genesis 1. God's blueprint for humanity was no less than for them to bear his likeness so that he could live within them, exercising his authority and blessing with and through his people.

2 Meeting on the mountain

Exodus 19:1–23

The intimate relationship depicted in Genesis 1, characterised by God indwelling his image, is short-lived. One need only turn the page to find the first instance of a theme which will become all too familiar in the pages which follow: humanity disregards God's command in pursuit of personal gain (Genesis 2—3). The terrible consequences culminate with the expulsion of the man and woman from the garden of Eden, and while this does not bar humanity from interacting with God, the rest of Genesis plays out with God known only from a distance.

It is only centuries later that God's intention to restore humanity to his presence comes into focus, when he reveals himself to Moses in a fire upon Mount Sinai (Exodus 3). By this time Israel was a subjugated people in Egypt, another renowned garden land (see Deuteronomy 11:10), and God sends Moses to confront Pharaoh and ensure a second expulsion from a garden, except this time they were to be expelled towards God's presence (Exodus 5—12). He led them through the wilderness back to Mount Sinai (Exodus 19), and there descended onto the mountaintop in an awe-inspiring display of storm, smoke and fire (vv. 18–19). This scene is typical of biblical encounters with the presence of God in all his glory, majesty and holiness (other examples include Deuteronomy 4:11; 2 Samuel 22:7–12; Ezekiel 1:4, 27).

At first, it seems that God's glory only emphasises the separation that must be maintained now that humanity lives outside the garden. The Israelites must wash their clothes and be consecrated (vv. 10–11) just to be within sight of God's glory, and they must remain at a distance (v. 12). And yet, so much of this passage is about giving Israel access to God. The people must be consecrated precisely so that they can see God's glory among them and receive the purpose he has for them: to be in covenant with him as his treasured people (v. 5), and to be a kingdom of priests (v. 6). A priest's life is lived in the presence of God. Indeed, a word-for-word translation of verse 22 tells of 'the priests, ones who come near to Yahweh'. Moses clearly understands this to mean the entire people (v. 23), since they are to become a kingdom of priests (v. 6). However, it is here that we reach the limits of God's as-yet-incomplete plan. Only Moses and Aaron can approach for now, emblems of a promise in its early stages of fulfilment.

3 Centred on God's presence

Exodus 40:34–38; 2 Chronicles 7:1–3

In the previous section, we reflected on the significance of Israel's encounter with God's presence on Mount Sinai in Exodus 19. The striking imagery used in that scene of God's presence manifested as fire is an ever-present theme throughout Israel's wilderness years, and it is particularly associated with God's guidance and protection (e.g. Exodus 13:21–22; 14:24), his judgement and atonement (e.g. Leviticus 9:24; 10:2), and the sheer majesty of his glory (e.g. Exodus 24:17). In these instances, the camera is pointed towards those who encounter God's glory and are transfixed and transformed by it.

Exodus closes with the dedication of the recently constructed tabernacle, in which the glory of the Lord descends in cloud and fire, as on Sinai (Exodus 40:34–38). Here, however, the emphasis is not on the transformative effect of God's glory (although we do again see God's guidance in view, vv. 36–37); instead, the camera is turned toward God himself, and we see both the unapproachable holiness of his glory and, at the same time, the astonishing access to his presence that he was giving to his people. Leviticus gives the closest attention to how such a paradox can be achieved, but for the writer of Exodus, the priority is that Israel knows that God intends to dwell among his people. More than that, as the final line of Exodus makes clear, he will go with them on the journey, so that 'the eyes of all the house of Israel' will see him (v. 38). It is not enough that he sees them; he wants to be seen.

Generations later, following the establishment of Israel in the promised land, King David's son Solomon commissioned a permanent temple to be built in Jerusalem as Israel's central place of worship. Once it was completed, Solomon led the prayers of dedication (2 Chronicles 6), and the Lord responded exactly as he had in Exodus 40. Once more, fire fell as the glory of the Lord filled the temple (literally 'house', 2 Chronicles 7:1); once more the priests were unable to enter the sanctuary because the glory of the Lord filled it (v. 2; see also 5:13–14). As in the wilderness, the fire of God was a sign of God's atoning forgiveness (note the sacrifices and the prayer that preceded them in 2 Chronicles 6), as well as an awesome revelation of himself and an assurance that he desired above all else to dwell in the midst of his people.

4 God's Spirit is with them

Ezekiel 11:14–21; 43:1–12

The years that followed the establishment of God's presence in the Jerusalem temple were turbulent to say the least. After Solomon's death, Israel descended into civil war and split into two kingdoms, Israel and Judah, both of which repeatedly rebelled against God by perpetuating idolatry and injustice. Eventually, the relationship between God and his people reached breaking point, ultimately resulting in God's people being overcome by the surrounding empires of Assyria and Babylon and taken into exile, away from the promised land and away from God's presence in the temple.

But that was not to be the end of the story. No sooner had God's judgement fallen than a new prophetic message began to emerge: God would restore his people. Isaiah and Jeremiah had both declared judgement, only to proceed to proclaim restoration and justice (Isaiah 40—55), a new covenant and forgiveness (Jeremiah 31—33). Zephaniah even proclaimed the return of the Lord's presence: 'Sing loud, O daughter Zion… The king of Israel, the Lord, is in your midst' (Zephaniah 3:14–15). The same themes run throughout Ezekiel, with the exiles' anguish about their separation from God at the heart of his message; Ezekiel 11:14–21 speaks directly to this anxiety. Although verse 15 frames this as an insight into what those who remained in Jerusalem were saying, what follows is intended as a word of comfort to the exiles. Contrary to appearances, the Lord *has* been with them in exile (v. 16), and now he promises to return them to the land (v. 17) and to give them a new united heart (v. 19), which would rejuvenate their faithfulness to God's law (v. 20). This description of restoration is arranged as a chiasm, which is to say that it has a centre point, around which are set mirrored themes, as follows:

A: The Lord will draw the exiles from the people (v. 17).
   B: In response, Judah will remove their idols (v. 18).
      C: The Lord will give them one heart (v. 19a)
         D: He will put a new spirit within them (v. 19b)
      C: The Lord will give them a heart of flesh (v. 19c)
   B: In response, Judah will follow God's law (v. 20a)
A: They will then become 'my people' (v. 20b)

At the heart of this chiasm is the promise that God will 'put a new spirit within them' (v. 19), and its placement here confirms that it is this that will enable

God's restoration of his people to his presence. This restoration is depicted vividly in Ezekiel's later vision of God's glory entering the new temple (Ezekiel 43:1–12) – a glory that Ezekiel describes as 'like the vision that I had seen by the river Chebar' (v.3) – that is, an inferno of cloud and fire (Ezekiel 1:4, 27). God's desire to live among his people had not abated and one day he would return in fire.

5 Once more the heavens will shake

Haggai 2:1–9; Zechariah 2:1–13

When God's people returned to the promised land after years of exile and began to rebuild the temple, it was an occasion both for rejoicing and weeping. Rejoicing the restoration this represented; weeping for the meagre scale of this second temple compared with the first. This is the context into which Haggai prophesies, and he directs his words to the disappointed: 'Who is left among you that saw this house in its former glory? How does it look to you now? Is it not in your sight as nothing?' (Haggai 2:3) To these people the Lord speaks courage, not because of who they are, but because *he is with them* (v. 5). Their strength is rooted in his presence. As in Ezekiel, Haggai connects God's presence with his spirit, but whereas Ezekiel had promised, 'he *will* put *a new spirit* within them' (Ezekiel 11:19, my italics), Haggai shifts tenses, from future to present continuous: God *is with them*. What now lies in the future is God's full return to his temple ('*I will* fill this house,' v. 7); an event which will also bring all the nations together under his sovereignty. Thus, Haggai's prophecy resonates with the promise first given to Abraham: 'In you all the families of the earth shall be blessed' (Genesis 12:3; compare Isaiah 2:2; Jeremiah 3:17; Micah 4:2; Zechariah 2:11).

A mere five months later, Zechariah the prophet proclaimed the imminent fulfilment of Haggai's words. In the third of a series of striking visions, he sees a man measuring Jerusalem in preparation for a new wall, which will be the Lord himself (Zechariah 2:1–5). As so often before, we find here the association of God's glory with fire, which on the one hand represents his protection, and on the other enables Jerusalem to be an open city, surrounded by a wall that makes space for all in a way that stone never could. However, the Lord would not only be the wall that surrounds the city; he would be the glory within it too (v. 5). Responding to this vision, Zechariah prophesied the return of God's presence, declaring twice: 'I will come and dwell in your midst' (Zechariah

2:10, 11b). Between these affirmations, he also prophesied the expansion of God's people, just as Haggai had done: 'Many nations shall join themselves to the Lord on that day' (v. 11a). God's promise had come into clearer focus: he would surround and dwell within his chosen people, who were to be made up of every nation.

6 Fire falls

Acts 2:1–21

Finally, we come to Pentecost, and we find the church gathered and waiting for the Holy Spirit as Jesus had commanded them (Acts 1:5, 8). The festival of Pentecost was also called the Festival of Weeks (Exodus 34:22; Leviticus 23:15–21; Numbers 28:26–31; Deuteronomy 16:9–12) and was one of three agricultural festivals at which the Israelites celebrated the fruitfulness of the earth. This association with the creational blessing of fruitfulness (Genesis 1:28), as well as the gift of the law at Sinai (Exodus 19:1), make this festival an appropriate backdrop to the gift of the Holy Spirit. Here too, we find a formative event inspired by a powerful encounter with the presence of God.

That this concerns God's presence is clear from the start. The sound of a violent wind from heaven (v. 2) evokes the storm from Exodus 19, and the detail that it 'filled the entire house' is strikingly reminiscent of 2 Chronicles 7:1, when the glory of the Lord 'filled the temple' (compare Exodus 40:34–35; 1 Kings 8:10–11; Isaiah 6:1). This is further impressed by Luke's reference to this venue as a 'house' (instead of 'upper room,' as in Acts 1:13), the same term used for the Jerusalem temple in the Old Testament. Indeed, as the fire falls into the house (v. 3), just as it had done in 2 Chronicles 7, and as the Holy Spirit fills the people (v. 4), just as the glory of the Lord had filled the temple, a direct connection is made to that momentous event. This first Pentecost for the church represented the fulfilment of the promises made through Ezekiel, Haggai and Zechariah; not only that, but it also redefined the church's understanding of its relationship with God's presence. From now on, God would dwell within them, just as he had first intended when he made humanity in his image in Genesis 1:26. In this sense, this scene brings one great arc of the biblical narrative to completion.

At the same time, this scene is also the beginning of the next phase in God's plan. The first act of the Holy Spirit was to empower the church to speak the language of 'every nation under heaven' (vv. 5, 9–11), in order to share 'God's deeds of power' (v. 11). Until this time, God's presence had been available in a limited way, but God's intention had always been to bless all nations (Genesis 12:3; Haggai 2:7; Zechariah 2:11). Peter, recalling the words of Joel, understood the significance: the Spirit had not come to give power to a select few. God's desire was to 'pour out my Spirit on all flesh' (v. 17; compare Joel 2:28). The calling on the church was to expand God's kingdom, so that 'everyone who calls on the name of the Lord shall be saved' (Acts 2:21; compare Joel 2:32).

Guidelines

Throughout this week we have explored the foundations of Pentecost in Acts 2. As we have seen, this momentous event represented both the completion of one aspect of God's plan and the commission of the church into another.

- Israel had first encountered God's presence in the pillar of cloud and fire, which led them through the wilderness, spoke to them at Sinai and lived among them first in the tabernacle and later in the Jerusalem temple. This was a mirage of the closeness God had intended at creation, which had been disrupted by humanity's continuous sinfulness, but it was still a vital step in God's plan for restoration. Centuries later, when the Holy Spirit fell as fire into the room where the early church was marking their first Pentecost together since the death and resurrection of Jesus, there was no mistaking the significance. Just as the cross had realised God's redemption of humanity from sin, the gift of the Holy Spirit was realising God's restoration of humanity to his presence. It is no wonder that years later, Peter drew on temple imagery to describe each Christian's place in the church: 'Like living stones, let yourselves be built into a spiritual house, to be a holy priesthood, to offer spiritual sacrifices acceptable to God through Jesus Christ' (1 Peter 2:5; compare 1 Corinthians 6:15–20). At Pentecost, God's plan to dwell within his people, exercising his sovereignty and blessing through them, had been accomplished.

- At the same time, however, there remained a vital limitation: namely that redemption and restoration from God emanate from relationship with God, and God's plan was not only to save those to whom he had previously related. His heart was for all people, and all nations. As such, the gift of the Spirit was more than a completion; it was also a commission. Christ's followers were to be witnesses of their own redemption and restoration and to expand the reaches of the kingdom so that 'everyone who calls on the name of the Lord shall be saved' (Acts 2:21; compare 1:5, 8).

- Thus, Pentecost is not only a time for celebration and thanksgiving in the church; it is also a time for reflection: do we engage with the Holy Spirit as God's presence with us, or do we view him as a distant mediator? And it is a time for recommitment to the church's calling to witness to the powerful acts of God.

FURTHER READING

Craig G. Bartholomew and Michael W. Goheen, *The Drama of Scripture: Finding our place in the biblical story* (SPCK, 2006).

Bryan D. Estelle, *Echoes of Exodus: Tracing a biblical motif* (IVP Academic, 2018).

Craig S. Keener, *Acts: An exegetical commentary, Volume 1* (Baker Academic, 2012).

David G. Peterson, *The Acts of the Apostles* (Apollos, 2009).

Sandra L. Richter, *The Epic of Eden: A Christian entry into the Old Testament* (IVP Academic, 2008).

Christopher J.H. Wright, *Knowing the Holy Spirit through the Old Testament* (Monarch, 2006).

The Holy Trinity

Nigel G. Wright

Following the Athanasian Creed, Christians believe in 'one God in Trinity, and Trinity in Unity… For there is one Person of the Father, another of the Son, and another of the Holy Spirit. But the godhead of the Father, of the Son, and of the Holy Spirit, is all one, the glory equal, the majesty co-eternal.' It continues, 'The Father incomprehensible, the Son incomprehensible, and the Holy Spirit incomprehensible', prompting one abbot, faced with preaching on Trinity Sunday, to exclaim, 'The whole darn thing incomprehensible!'

But is it? Our understanding of God *has to be* 'incomprehensible' once we also say that God is infinite, unfathomable and mysterious. The peace of God 'transcends all understanding' (Philippians 4:7), but so does God's very self. It is one thing to know God by grace through faith and entirely another to say we know *what it is to be God*. We are too limited even to understand the universe and our own selves, let alone the one who created all things. Modesty and humility are in order. Yet we also believe in *revelation*, God's gracious initiative in making God's own self known. The record of this revelation is to be found in both Old Testament and New Testament, gaining pace as it proceeds and reaching its climax in the one who is the Word of God (John 1:1, 14), the image and 'exact representation' of God's being (Hebrews 1:1–3). Beyond that there is the ultimate future: now we know in part but then we shall know as we ourselves have been known (1 Corinthians 13:12–13). Only on the basis of revelation may we speak with confidence about God; and what we have to say is both extraordinary and revolutionary.

The studies that follow aim to clarify some key biblical passages that guide us on this particular path (there are many more texts). We begin with the Old Testament emphasis on God's unity – there is one God – and then lead into the New Testament insistence that this same God is Father, Son and Spirit. Our aim is to grow in understanding but even more to worship. Albert Einstein wrote, 'Everything should be made as simple as possible – but no simpler.' This advice we seek to follow.

Unless otherwise stated, Bible quotations are taken from the NIV.

1 God our creator

Genesis 1

The beginning is not a bad place to begin! Everything has its beginning in God, who wills to create that which is not God. God creates matter and then proceeds to give it shape and order. God then lays creation under a necessity to flourish and realise its potential, to be fruitful and multiply. This is a wonderful and worshipful celebration of God's creativity. It is notable both for what it says and what it (implicitly) denies.

For instance, it denies atheism. It denies that there are many gods of equal importance (polytheism) – instead there is only one God, who is all-important. It denies that the world is itself God (pantheism), since it is simply something the transcendent God has made. It further denies paganism, since the sun, moon and stars are not deities to be worshipped but lights that mark the times (vv. 14–19). Moreover, it denies that God is some kind of impersonal, ultimate power round which the world revolves, since the God of creation is decidedly personal: this God speaks, wills and purposes, takes pleasure in what is made and pronounces the world to be good. These are the major affirmations of the chapter. Furthermore, there is within creation something that can reflect God and it exists in the form of human beings, male and female, who are personal and relational and can imitate God in acting as stewards (v. 26). God is way beyond any kind of limit that is true of human beings or the created order, yet we are talking of a personal Creator, and such a God can not only create but love and care for what is made. We are not living in an uncaring world. And this personal God is one, the ultimate reality that gives all things being.

Yet there are hints here of more to come. 'And God said' is seven times repeated. God speaks and so goes out of God's own self into the world by means of word and breath (see also Psalm 33:6–9). In Hebrew 'breath', 'wind' and 'spirit' are all the same word (*ruach*) and verse 2 says, 'The Spirit of God was hovering [or sweeping] over the waters.' God's word and God's Spirit will prove to be important insights into the personal God's own being, as we shall see.

2 God defines God

G.K. Chesterton claimed, 'God made human beings in his own image – and they have been returning the compliment ever since.' When we make God look like us, we promote our own interests. Sometimes the result is ugly; at other times it is simply weak.

This passage does not allow us to do this. The God of Abraham (v. 15) is the one who takes the initiative in redeeming fallen humanity, choosing Abraham and his descendants as the vehicle for reaching all nations (Genesis 12:1–3). The strategy is to form a people whose understanding of God's ways will be a revelation and blessing to all people. After Abraham, the pivotal figure is Moses, a mediator and liberator, and this passage speaks of the crucial encounter between him and God at the burning bush. Typically, gods have a name and Moses needs to know with whom he is dealing. So God defines himself: 'I am who I am' (or possibly 'I will be what I will be'). God is sovereign, self-disclosing and self-defining, not to be controlled, manipulated or turned into some projection of the human imagination. God is not an object to be possessed by us but an eternal subject in whose presence we are on holy ground (v. 5). Like Moses, we are humbled and awestruck in the presence of the Lord (v. 6).

God's name, Yahweh, is so holy that Jewish readers substitute for it the word 'Adonai', or LORD, and bow as they do so. God has weight, and so it should be. Yet the name implies that who God is will be discovered only as we relate in worship, prayer and obedience to the divine subject. As the God who began a work with Abraham and continues it with Moses, saving the Israelites from slavery and leading them into the land where they will be free to be God's treasured possession (Exodus 19:3–6), so who God is will be more perfectly disclosed. This is an unfinished story.

We do well to 'fear' the God who is holy, not in a cringing way but in a way that is clean, pure and reverent. And behind this is the quiet confidence, as Moses discovered, that the Lord is 'the compassionate and gracious God, slow to anger, abounding in love and faithfulness' (Exodus 34:6–7).

3 The Lord is one

Jewish believers have a prayer for each morning and evening. It is here in verses 4–5 and is known as the 'Shema', the Hebrew word for 'hear' with which it begins. When asked which is the most important commandment in the law, Jesus chose this (Matthew 22:34–40).

In this passage, instructions were given that made sure the prayer was deeply embedded in Jewish devotion. It was to be internalised in their hearts, taught to their children, spoken of along the way, bound to their foreheads, inscribed on their doorposts (vv. 6–9). Why be so emphatic? The reason is to do with loyalty. Obedience to God's ways has nothing to do with servility (as modern people tend to assume) and everything to do with loyalty and love. We are to love God and to love doing the will of God. The chief charge of Israel's later prophets against kings and people alike was the problem of divided loyalty, the wilfulness that strayed from covenant faithfulness to the Lord to worship other gods. When it says 'the Lord is one', its primary meaning is that for God's people there is only one who matters and there are no rivals. Precisely because we tend to wander, the unique and exclusive claims of this God need to define who God's people are at a deep and instinctive level.

It is probable that when Israel did indeed stray towards other gods, they did not understand things this way. It is not that they chose other gods instead of the Lord, but that they wanted to swing both ways, to have the Lord *and* the other gods as a form of insurance, just in case. Surrounded by nations that had no loyalty to Israel's God, they found it easy to fall into line or be carried along by the pressures of their environment. Not much has changed. We can all detect in ourselves the power that other gods that are not gods can exert on us (Galatians 4:8). We do well to remember that the oneness of God is indeed a doctrine and yet much more besides: it represents an existential position, an attitude to what counts in life. It is the confidence that we need look nowhere else but the Lord.

4 Monotheism?

Some think that early Israelites were not strictly monotheistic, that is, committed to the philosophical belief that there is only one God. Other nations were welcome to their gods, but Israel owed exclusive loyalty to Yahweh (for instance, Micah 4:5). In time the clear conviction arose that there is indeed only one God: 'I am God, and there is no other; I am God and there is none like me' (v. 9). That Israel's God is incomparable is reinforced by the biting satire about dumb idols that we find in verses 5–7 and in 44:6–20. There is one God not only for Israel but for all the world.

Monotheism comes in for regular criticism. Is it not a form of imperialism, a claim to domination? Can it not be used to support unaccountable monarchs or dictators? Is it not potentially intolerant in denying the validity of other pathways, other versions of 'god'? On the other hand, belief in one God also leads to the conviction that we live in one world in which everything is connected: there is a fundamental interdependence between things. Furthermore, there is one humanity made in God's image in which beneath the distinctions of race, gender, culture, nationality and much else there is an essential unity to be nurtured. 'From one man [literally: blood] [God] made all the nations that they should inhabit the whole earth' (Acts 17:26). One God, one world, one humanity (see Malachi 2:10). With all our diversity, which is to be celebrated, there is a harmony to be realised – because of one God. Monotheism is good news.

Of course, in trusting in one God, everything depends on what this God is like. A supreme deity that is impersonal, or cruel, punitive and overbearing, is not good news. One who is 'compassionate and gracious' and also resolutely resists evil (Exodus 34:4–7) is no threat to the world but its very hope. Far from legitimating the cruel and domineering, such a God calls all abusive behaviour into question. Probably Jesus had this in mind when he said, 'And do not call anyone on earth "father", for you have one Father, and he is in heaven' (Matthew 23:9).

But there is a question: what does it mean for God to be one?

5 The Lord takes form

Genesis 18:1–8, 16–33

Although the name of Yahweh was later revealed to Moses, already in this incident, Yahweh (the Lord) is appearing to Abraham. The name occurs often (vv. 1, 13, 17, 19, 26, 33). Yet it is all very mysterious. God appears as the Lord, but also as a man, or three men. In 19:1 two of these men are described as 'angels'. The language slips between the Lord, men and angels and leaves us perplexed. That it is a divine encounter is not in doubt, but it is a strange one, and what might it tell us about God, and particularly about divine unity and three-ness?

Some see an early trace of the Trinity, but we should be cautious. God who created the world has ways of 'taking form' within it when communicating with those he chooses. Here, three men embody the Lord. Later, Jacob will wrestle with a 'man' at Peniel and afterwards pronounce 'I saw God face to face' (32:30). Repeatedly in the Old Testament the 'angel of the Lord' or 'of God' acts in the world. God, seemingly, has the power to project God's own self into the world through mediators. And why not? God is God and can freely choose to take form in achieving the divine purpose. This is the living God, and without there being some kind of mediator we would not be able to bear the sight or sound of God (Exodus 20:18–19). Already in Genesis 1 we saw that God brings the world into being through his word and by his Spirit. To these insights we may make reference to God's glory (1 Kings 8:11), God's presence (Exodus 33:14) and God's wisdom (Proverbs 8), all of which are extensions of the reality that is God in the world and seem to have a semi-independent, and in the case of Wisdom a personified, existence. The oneness of God is not all that needs to be identified in the Old Testament. There is also a vitality, a fullness, an energy that shows it is not enough to think of Israel's God as a solitary monad. More has to be thought and said.

So we turn to the New Testament. A saying will guide us: 'In the Old the New Testament is concealed. In the New the Old is revealed'.

6 Father, Son, Spirit

Matthew 3

Early in the New Testament we encounter an important scenario. Jesus comes to John the Baptist to be baptised in the Jordan. As he comes up from the water, the Spirit of God descends upon him and a voice from heaven pronounces 'This is my Son, whom I love' (vv. 16–17). The New Testament develops from this point. Notice that it is not that the Father now appears in a different guise as the Son. Nor is it that Father and Son then become the Spirit. All three 'persons' of the Trinity exist together in close and responsive relationship. There is purposeful interaction between the three. This leads us to develop how we understand God's work in our space and time and, even more, how we are to think of God's very nature.

God's revelation of God's own self increases over time. The declaration that 'I will be what I will be' (Exodus 3:14) means that Yahweh (I AM!), the one and only God, is disclosed to us progressively through divine acts which are then interpreted in the words of the prophets. With the coming of Jesus as the Son of God we reach a whole new stage. In Luke 10:22 we hear Jesus saying, 'No one knows who the Son is except the Father, and no one knows who the Father is except the Son and those to whom the Son chooses to reveal him.' Jesus the Son mediates the knowledge of the Father and does so uniquely. Through him others can enter into such knowledge. His role is pivotal. We now have to think new thoughts about God.

Let us be clear: this does not mean that in the Old Testament only God the Father existed, then with his conception God the Son was created, then on the day of Pentecost the Holy Spirit came into being. Nor is it as though first God wears the mask of Father, then changes the mask to become the Son and yet another to become the Spirit. Rather, who God is and has always been in eternity becomes known to us as God's work of revelation unfolds through time. The truth is more wonderful than we could imagine: our God has three ways of being God.

Guidelines

In the world of Christian belief we are often asked to hold two contrasting thoughts together and to accept that the truth lies in the tension between them. We believe that creation is both good and fallen, that human beings are essentially good but actually estranged, that God's kingdom is now but not yet, that the scriptures are human words but contain God's word, that Jesus is both fully God and fully human, that salvation is both a gift and a task. The point is that the full truth is not in either one end or the other but in both at the same time. Indeed, to over-emphasise one end rather than the other is to go astray. So it is with the Holy Trinity: God is both one and three. To lean one way would be to say that a singular God progressively wears three masks (this is known as 'modalism'). To lean the other would be to imagine that there are three individual 'Gods' (known as 'tritheism'). The truth is that there is precisely one God who is Father, Son and Spirit.

Even before the doctrine of the Trinity was formulated, Christians already worshipped the Father through the Son and in the Spirit. The doctrine was clarified in order to explain why it is that they did so. It is often pointed out, quite rightly, that the word 'Trinity' never appears in the New Testament, and so some are reluctant to use it. But there is good reason for the word: it captures the core reality of Christian worship, prayer and the experience of salvation. From the beginning Christians have encountered the reality that is God the Father through and because of Christ the Son and by means of the Holy Spirit. So: 'For through him [Christ] we both [Jews and Gentiles] have access to the Father by one Spirit' (Ephesians 2:18). This is the essence of Christian faith and it is experiential and trinitarian. First of all, we know God through Christ and the Spirit, and become those who 'participate in the divine nature' (2 Peter 1:4). This experience, rooted in God's self-revelation, then shapes the way we think and speak: enter the doctrine of the Trinity. What follows explains this more fully.

1 God incarnate

John 1:1–18

This passage is hugely important. Imagine Christ as the key that unlocks 'all the treasures of wisdom and knowledge' (Colossians 2:3). Here this means the mysteries of creation (v. 3), of humankind (v. 14), of salvation (vv. 12–13), but most significantly of God's very being: 'No one has ever seen God, but the one and only Son… has made him known' (v. 18). He himself is God, now made incarnate as a human being, who has been with God from the beginning and is God's very Word (vv. 1–2). *Someone* has been made incarnate, not something. Christ is the full expression of God's being and the communication of that being to those who behold his glory (v. 14), the glory of the unique Son. He is God but as the Son of the Father he is not the Father. Because he himself is truly God he can show us what God is truly like. So we are presented with a paradox: alongside the one God there is another who is also God and always has been.

Some resolve the paradox by saying that the Son is a kind of secondary deity. Or perhaps being called God is a form of courtesy title. But these interpretations will not do. For a start Isaiah 46:9 proclaims, 'I am God, *and there is no other*' (my italics). Then again, when it comes to being God there is no half-way house; it is not possible in biblical terms to be a subsidiary or demi-god. Furthermore, the language here is entirely clear: 'the Word was

52

God'. This serves as an introduction to the gospel as a whole in which Christ can declare, 'Before Abraham was born, I am!' (8:58–59). Christ shared the Father's glory before the world began (17:5). John then repeatedly records the so-called 'I am' sayings in which Christ takes to himself the name of Yahweh as revealed in Exodus 3:14 (6:35, 8:12, 10:7, 10:11, 11:25, 14:6, 15:1). In Christ, God takes form supremely as Jesus of Nazareth and so continues to define God's own self.

John begins his gospel with a statement about the identity of the Christ and ends it equally clearly. In 20:28 Thomas confesses the risen Christ with the words, 'My Lord and my God!' Our understanding of the one God is being re-defined.

2 The second difference

John 14:15–31

According to John 1 there is both a unity of Father and Son and a difference between them. In this chapter we find a second difference between the Spirit and the Son, and therefore also with the Father. Yet this is a 'differentiated unity' and in no sense a separation: one God, three persons. To appreciate this fully, we will need to make a brief excursion into the underlying Greek.

The distinction-in-unity between Father and Son comes clearly through this chapter once more (vv. 9–14). And we are now made aware of the second difference: the Father will give 'another advocate to help you and be with you forever – the Spirit of truth' (vv. 16–17). The word 'advocate' translates *paraclete*, which means one who is called alongside to help and so could also be 'counsellor' or 'helper'. Jesus is going away but will come back (vv. 18, 28) in the form of the Spirit.

The word 'another' in verse 16 is particularly interesting. Like other languages, Greek distinguishes between 'other' in the sense of 'other and different' (*heteros*) and 'other' meaning 'other and the same' (*allos*). The Spirit of truth is *another of the same kind* as Jesus (*allos parakletos*) and this has immense significance: the Spirit is the same as Jesus in being truly and fully God, and is also personal – the Spirit 'will teach you all things and will remind you of everything I have said to you' (v. 26). These are personal actions, not those of an impersonal force. 16:12–15 adds to this by saying the Spirit will guide the disciples into all the truth and will glorify Christ. It is striking here that the original Greek breaks grammatical rules by using a masculine pronoun to refer to a neuter noun (*pneuma*) and so stresses the personhood of the Spirit. God's Spirit is someone, not something. We are shaping a doctrine of the Trinity.

Yet is there a problem? Jesus both says, 'I and the Father are one' (10:30) and 'the Father is greater than I' (14:28). Philippians 2:5–11 can clarify this by distinguishing between Christ 'being in very nature God' and his 'taking the very nature of a servant'. As God there is equality; as 'flesh' (1:14) there is humility. Christ is God incarnate.

3 Going deep

1 Corinthians 2:6–16

The Holy Spirit has been said to be the neglected person of the Trinity. The results of neglect are always serious. We might pray of the Father, 'The Lord make his face shine on you' (Numbers 6:24–26). We might fairly imagine the face of Jesus, the incarnate one. But we cannot imagine the Spirit having a face, so the Spirit tends to be more anonymous. Moreover, the Spirit has also been described as 'God in his reticence', more apt to speak of Christ and the Father and to glorify them (John 16:13–14) than to draw attention to himself. We are guilty of neglect when we do not honour the Spirit as we should.

This passage certainly does not neglect God's Spirit. The Spirit knows God exhaustively (v. 11) and so can communicate God to us. The Spirit knows the mind of Christ and so can impart this to us (v. 16). Nothing less than God can fathom God and nothing less than God can adequately reveal God. There is an analogy and a logic here. The analogy is with a person's spirit or interior self (v. 11): nobody can know other persons except those persons themselves. Our spirits know the deep things that are interior to us. We might fairly object that sometimes we are a mystery to ourselves, and that would be true, but Paul's analogy holds. God's Spirit knows everything that is to be known of the unfathomable God, and to do this must be at one with and equal to the Father and the Son. God's Spirit is eternal (Hebrews 9:14).

The logic must follow that it is truly possible to know God. God the Father is the source of all that is. The Father is made known to us by the incarnate Son who is 'the radiance of God's glory and the exact representation of his being' (Hebrews 1:3). Yet Father and Son are known to us through God the Spirit 'that we may understand what God has freely given us' (2:12). God's Spirit might therefore be thought of as God at God's closest to us, the one who can transform us into God's image (2 Corinthians 3:17–18). Honouring the Spirit honours Father and Son.

4 Time and eternity

Ephesians 1:3–14

The Trinity is not a mathematical puzzle but the summary of a story. Scripture is the witness to the 'greatest story ever told'. This passage gives us the big picture stretching from before the creation to the final redemption of all things. It is the story of a divine purpose with its origin in God the Father that is entirely good, gracious and unimaginably generous (vv. 3–5). That purpose has always had its centre in the chosen one we know as Jesus Christ, God's Son, our Lord (v. 9). He is God's greatest gift and in him are found redemption and forgiveness, made available to us in that he has lived our life and died our death. He makes available 'sonship', which has little to do with gender and everything to do with inheritance (vv. 5, 14). Everything that is his, and that is everything, is destined to become ours. Christians have experienced 'adoption' through him, that is, they have entered in the here and now into a relationship with the Father that grants us favour, blessing and new life. We are more than servants: we are God's very children, brothers and sisters of Jesus himself. Yet this is just the beginning, because we have a hope that stretches into the ultimate future, one which imagines everything being brought back into harmony through Christ. If the Father is the creator, then the Son is the re-creator of all things (v. 10).

The story is still in progress. It is being realised in the present age through the Holy Spirit, God at his closest to us, sealing us as God's own possession as a down-payment and guarantee of all that is yet to come (v. 14). The Spirit may then be called the 'trans-creator' or transformer who has been active throughout the whole story and brings to completion what has been purposed by the Father and accomplished by the Son in an expanding forward-movement that will only be complete when God is all in all (1 Corinthians 15:28).

This story is everywhere in the New Testament. In it we see who God is. God works in this triune way in time because this is who God is, has always been and always will be, in eternity. And in this revelation God speaks the truth about God's own self.

5 God's name

Throughout the Bible God is spoken of through many images and metaphors. Specific titles are ascribed to God, such as El Elyon or 'God Most High' (Genesis 14:18–20), and El Shaddai or 'God Almighty' (Genesis 17:1). But a name is more than a title. In Hebrew thought, a person's name expressed their very essence, who they were – far more than a convenient label. As a person developed in significance, their name might change to indicate the fact, as in the case of Abram becoming Abraham (Genesis 17:4–8) or Jacob's becoming Israel (Genesis 32:27–28). In Exodus 3 we witnessed the Lord revealing his own preferred name to Moses, 'I Am Who I Am'. This is an enduring name (3:15) which we continue to honour. But the name can also be translated, 'I Will Be What I Will Be'. God's self-revelation was not complete with Moses but was to continue until its clearest point was reached in Jesus, God's Son.

Matthew 28:19–20 contains the so-called 'baptismal formula', the name of God in which those who enter the Christian faith and the church are baptised. By using this name when it baptises, the church identifies the meaning of the act of baptism: it is about becoming a participant in the story of Father, Son and Spirit and benefitting from the grace of God that is made available through this good news. In this sense, baptism is a defining moment that orientates a person in a certain direction and defines who God intends them to be. For this reason, the water speaks of cleansing from sin and the burial of the past in order to rise with Christ to new life (Romans 6:1–4).

We notice, however, that there is only one name and in that one name Father, Son and Spirit are contained. There is one divine reality and it is made known to us in three ways. It has to be this way precisely because this is who God is in eternity – one God with three ways of being God. These are no competing or independent agents but one God who works out one purpose in utter harmony and agreement, never to be divided. God is a communion of loving persons and invites fallen and broken creatures to enjoy him forever.

6 Benediction

Acts of worship are incomplete without a benediction. In Numbers 6:22–27 the Aaronic priests were commissioned to 'put my name on the Israelites' by proclaiming the blessing over them. So Christians continue to do, often by using 'the grace' as found in verse 14 of today's reading. Divine blessing involves Father, Son and Spirit. 'Grace', 'love' and 'fellowship' could characterise each of the three persons, but it is significant how they are attributed. *Grace* is revealed to us in Christ in that through him God's unmerited favour overcomes sin and death. *Love* has its eternal origin in the heart of God the Father, the source of all, and is an ultimate reality. *Fellowship* refers to the Holy Spirit since the Spirit binds us together in ways that reflect the loving bonds of Father, Son and Spirit. God not only shows love but *is* love (1 John 4:16). Love is the essence of God's being. Since love is an interpersonal experience, we are entitled to believe that before God loved the world there was love without measure between Father, Son and Spirit in eternity (Ephesians 3:14–19). Love overflows and love binds 'all together in perfect unity' (Colossians 3:14).

Having stressed the divinity of each person of the Trinity, it strikes us here that the Father is specifically referred to as 'God'. We can infer that within God's being, as in all things, there is a kind of order which proceeds from Father to Son to Spirit, and so places the Father in the role of 'source and origin' of Son and Spirit. This is strengthened in that the Son is 'begotten' by the Father, even if 'eternally begotten', and that the Spirit is said to 'go out' or proceed from the Father (John 15:26). Does this make the Son or Spirit less fully God than the Father? The answer to this must be quite the opposite. This is the language of mutual dependence, of holy communion and belonging together, of mutual service and blessing, not the language of power hierarchies – however awesomely powerful the sovereign Lord might happen to be. It is the dynamic of self-giving love which is the very nature of God. Such love has gone out from God to embrace us too, through the Son by the Spirit.

Guidelines

I listened on the radio to someone explaining her happy discovery that God was actually 'three people'. Seemingly she was unaware of the bundle of misconceptions involved. To be fair, in this area it is easy to say the wrong thing or even the right thing in the wrong way. But we owe it to God and ourselves to speak as clearly as possible. God is not any kind of 'people', let alone three. God is God, of an incomparable and utterly unique order from created reality.

God is one, Trinity not troika! There is one God with one mind, one will, one purpose, one consciousness and one nature. This unity is expressed in three ways of being God, as Father, Son and Spirit, an eternal communion of being that is revealed to us in the works and words of God witnessed in the scriptures and supremely in the person of Christ. There are no conflicts or contradictions in God but only one united purpose in the creation, reconciliation and redemption of the world. Trinity Sunday, celebrated last week, represents the high point of the whole of the Christian year in which annually we travel through the seasons of Nativity, Epiphany, Lent, Good Friday and Easter, Ascension and Pentecost. The vision of God that emerges from all these celebrations is of God who is both one and three.

In the end, when we have thought our best thoughts, we return to where it all began, in the worship of the Father through the Son and in the Spirit that we find in the New Testament. 'God sent the Spirit of his Son into our hearts, the Spirit who calls out "*Abba*, Father"' (Galatians 4:6). Equally, 'no one can say "Jesus is Lord," except by the Holy Spirit' (1 Corinthians 12:3). This is the language of worship. It continues today in doxologies such as 'Glory to the Father and to the Son and to the Holy Spirit, as it was in the beginning, is now and ever shall be'. Father, Son and Spirit are together to be worshipped and glorified because they are truly worthy as the one God, and 'from him and through him and for him are all things. To him be the glory forever! Amen' (Romans 11:36).

FURTHER READING

Edward Dunzl, *A Brief History of the Doctrine of the Trinity in the Early Church* (T. and T. Clark, 2007).

Roger E. Olson, *The Mosaic of Christian Belief* (Apollos, 2002), chapter 6.

Fred Sanders, *The Deep Things of God: How the Trinity changes everything* (Crossway, 2017).

Nigel G. Wright, *God on the Inside* (BRF, 2006).

Nigel G. Wright, *Vital Truth: The convictions of the Christian community* (Lutterworth, 2015), chapters 2 and 3.

Genesis 37—43:
the Joseph cycle

Ashley Hibbard

The portion of Genesis commonly called 'the Joseph cycle', Genesis 37—50, is one of the most unique sets of narrative in scripture. Rich in detail, dialogue and character development, with a compelling plot containing betrayal, intrigue and even sacrifice, some have called it more a novella than a set of independent narratives. While some have perceived it as a set of stories not originally belonging to the patriarchal narratives of Genesis, but rather poorly grafted on to the end, upon careful examination these stories fit quite well with many of the themes that both precede and follow, such as family dysfunction, sojourning in foreign lands, deliverance from foreign powers and God's sovereign control and divine guidance over human history.

In these next two weeks, we'll look at the first half of the Joseph cycle, Genesis 37—43 (we will study the next half in the following issue of *Guidelines*). The narratives in this section range in popularity from some of the best-loved to most ignored texts in scripture. But more importantly, they help us to understand what led to one of the key periods in the formative stage of Israel's history: the 400 years of slavery in Egypt. These texts are not just brilliantly told literature, but absolutely crucial theology as they bring us one step closer to the exodus from Egypt, the Old Testament's paradigmatic salvation story.

Unless otherwise stated, Bible quotations are taken from the ESV.

1 A downhill spiral

Genesis 37:1–11

There are few more recognisable scenes from the Old Testament than Joseph's receipt of a 'coat of many colours' from his father. Immortalised in movies, plays and Sunday school white boards, it is nonetheless only one of the reasons for which Joseph is hated by his brothers. It is reasonable to think that their hatred was not entirely irrational, as in the first matter of contention (v. 2) it is strongly implied that Joseph has been attempting to get his brothers in trouble. Two items in the text support this: first, while nearly all major translations say something like 'Joseph was pasturing the flock with his brothers', the most natural sense of the grammar would be to invert those two objects: 'Joseph was pasturing his brothers with the sheep.' This would suggest that it is far more his brothers with whom he is concerned than the flock.

Second, this 'report' that Joseph takes to his father could well be translated 'gossip'. It is not at all the usual word for 'message' or 'report', and though it is quite rare in the Hebrew Bible, it seems often to carry a connotation of a message that is slanted or less than truthful. And so with Joseph not only seeking to get his brothers in trouble, but apparently being rewarded for it, perhaps their hatred of him begins to make some sense.

The nature of this reward is somewhat unclear. It is evidently a unique garment that marked him out in some way. The traditional translation of 'coat of many colours' was first used in the Septuagint and perpetuated in the Vulgate. The Hebrew is less clear and may mean something like, 'a coat of palms' (hand, not tree) or perhaps 'a coat of spreading' (referring to size or length). If this is correct, then the sense would be a garment that had sleeves or that was long, and therefore not appropriate for labouring in a field.

Narratively, a third point of contention between Joseph and his brothers would seem fitting, and so it appears to be a point of emphasis that the third matter of contention comes in two parts. This is the first of three pairs of prophetic dreams that Joseph will interpret, and each interpretation will be the catalyst for a change in Joseph's status, as we will see in the following text.

2 The murdered brother

Genesis 37:12–36

In the first half of this story, we saw four reasons for which Joseph was hated by his brothers. It may be a matter of narrative symmetry that in the second half of the story we see four movements of Joseph, as in very short order his position changes from the favoured son of a powerful nomad to a slave being trafficked to a foreign land. This scene opens similarly to the prior one, with Joseph sent by his father to check on both his brothers and the sheep.

Joseph's encounter with an unnamed man at Dothan has been the matter of some interest. Details in Hebrew narrative are rarely superfluous, particularly where dialogue is involved, but the significance of this brief scene is unclear. The Samaritan Pentateuch suggests that it is not a man that he encounters but rather an angel, perhaps an effort to align this scene with the divine appointment motif in the Joseph cycle. More likely, though, is that it serves to raise the narrative tension: had Joseph not encountered someone who knew where his brothers had gone after Dothan, he might not have found them and thus returned home, safe under his father's watchful eye.

His brothers' inclination to kill him does not appear to be overly sudden or rash. The text states that they see him and start this discussion 'before he came near to them'. They throw him in a dry well, planning to leave him there to die. This is not only an exceptionally cruel way to kill him – to let him die of thirst, rather than to kill him quickly – but also is short-sighted and irresponsible. What is now a dry well will in the rainy season be a much-needed watering hole in the wilderness. If Joseph dies there, any water in there will be contaminated for quite some time.

In the end, the brothers choose to sell him to a trade caravan, and they pretend that this is better than murdering him (v. 27). But for Joseph, stripped literally of his coat and figuratively of his position, his family, his country and even his freedom, there is little difference. His brothers seek to remove him from the family, and, for all intents and purposes, they appear to have succeeded.

3 An impossible situation

Genesis 37 shows a family thrown into chaos, first through a father's favouritism and then through his sons' sinful reaction to the situation. Genesis 38 shows how this dissolution continues, and in fact is perpetuated to the next generation. As the story opens, Judah 'went down' from his brothers. Given the unity that the brothers demonstrated in the prior chapter in their hatred for Joseph, perhaps this movement away from them is a demonstration of the fact that being unified by sin and lies is much less enduring than unification around peace and truth.

In this chapter, it appears that Judah doesn't just live among the Canaanites, but that he becomes thoroughly 'Canaanised'. He has a Canaanite wife, an apparently Canaanite daughter-in-law and sons who are considered so wicked that God kills them directly, which is, notably, the only time that God appears in the story.

Judah's command to Onan to father a child on behalf of his dead brother is a practice seen in a variety of ancient Near Eastern sources. In a culture where lineage and inheritance were paramount, it was a way of ensuring that the family lines of those who died unexpectedly were not lost, and perhaps was also intended to ensure that the widow, likely very young if she had not yet had a child, was cared for. Historically, many commentators have tried to draw a moral lesson about irregular sexual activity from this passage, but this misses the emphasis on motive: twice in verse 9, it is stated that Onan did not want to provide for his brother's inheritance. It appears that God killed him for pretending to honour his father's request and father a child on behalf of his brother. This was a matter of economics, not sex.

While the reader is told that Er and Onan's deaths have been caused by God, the characters do not know that. Judah is faced with two dead sons, who both died after marrying the same woman. Judah's lie to Tamar is perhaps understandable, but his actions are cruel. By telling her to live *as a widow* in her father's house, he does not release her from her obligation to his family so that she can find another husband, but neither does he keep her nearby. She is stuck in a sort of social catch-22, neither cared for by Judah nor freed from his family.

4 The right (wrong) thing to do

Genesis 38:12–30

Whether or not Tamar realised immediately that Judah was attempting to rid himself of an unlucky woman, she appears to figure it out and form a plan, awaiting only an opportunity. That opportunity comes in the form of an extremely brief piece of information: only six words in the Hebrew: 'Your father-in-law is going up to Timnah to shear his sheep.'

This narrative centres around the execution of this plan, bookended by Tamar's change in garment: first, from honourable widow to dishonourable prostitute, and then back again after she has enacted her plan successfully. There has been some disagreement over whether this ostensibly commercial sexual encounter may be considered 'levirate'. On the one hand, it is of course not a literal brother-in-law. But both the Middle Assyrian laws and the Hittite legal code suggest that if the dead man had no brothers, his father or uncle could fulfil the function of the brother-in-law.

Tamar's request for payment is expected, of course, as she is posing as a prostitute, but it is striking that the pledge that she requests has a worth that far outweighs a mere goat kid. Functionally, she has asked for his credit card and car keys, and Judah's easy acceptance of this probably is intended to portray Judah as impulsive and rash. Of course, she never wanted the goat, only the items by which she could later identify Judah as the father.

This becomes critical, as when Judah learns that she is pregnant, he calls for her to be burned. This is striking, because stoning is the typical means of execution in the Hebrew Bible. The Talmud suggests that death by burning is the most extreme form of capital punishment that may be used. For Judah to call for this penalty may be an indication that he has come to think very highly of himself as a community leader, and certainly makes it all the more ironic when Tamar reveals that he is in fact the father of her unborn child.

Having officially identified his staff and seal, Judah concludes that Tamar is more righteous than he is. While he acknowledges that he did not give her his third son for a husband, exactly how that ranks below prostitution is unclear. It seem probable that Judah sees that Tamar has accepted this degrading role in order to fulfil her obligation to bear children for his family and to secure her own future. While her actions have secured her future, she has not been solely self-seeking as Judah has been.

5 The Lord was with Joseph

Genesis 39

Following the interlude of Genesis 38, we return to Joseph enslaved in Egypt in Genesis 39. This is the second occurrence of a pattern throughout Joseph's life, where he rises to the highest attainable position of authority in whatever situation he finds himself. His father marked him out as special with a garment that likely implied authority. Now in Potiphar's house he is a slave, but he rises in prominence until he is the chief of Potiphar's slaves. Whatever the earthly means, this is clearly the result of divine favour. The chapter is bookended with the phrase 'The Lord was with Joseph' (vv. 2, 23), and the author makes it clear that it is God's blessing of Joseph's diligence that brings him the trust of his master.

This phrase 'The Lord was with Joseph' is rather striking, as references to Yahweh have become fewer in the latter part of Genesis. God is utterly absent from Genesis 34 (Dinah and Shechem) and 37, and only appears in 38 to bring death to Er and Onan. Since gods in the ancient Near East were often perceived as territorial, it might make a certain amount of sense for that trend to continue. But on the contrary, we are told twice that God is with Joseph, even when Joseph is alone, even when he is far from the land that has been promised to his family, even when he is a slave. It is perhaps the first of many indications throughout the Old Testament that the God of the Hebrews is indeed the God of a people group, not a location.

It is intriguing that after Potiphar hears his wife's well-rehearsed story, the text says, 'his anger was kindled', but it does not directly state the object of his anger. It is very possible that it is not Joseph with whom he is angry, but rather his wife. Had Potiphar believed his wife, nothing would have prevented him from killing a slave who he considered a danger to his family. But for Joseph to end up imprisoned with important political prisoners suggests that Potiphar has a sense that his wife is lying, but is removing Joseph to save face. Regardless, once more we see that even here, Joseph finds himself moved into a position of authority, thought well of by the warden. However bleak Joseph's prospects may seem, his God can continue to bless him in the most unlikely and unjust places.

6 The second pair of dreams

Genesis 40

In this chapter, we come to the second pair of dreams in the Joseph cycle, the interpretations of which will, eventually, result in Joseph's release from prison. Despite the humiliating circumstances in which Joseph finds himself, incarcerated for a crime that he did not commit, he appears to have maintained not only a generic faith in God, but even the confidence that God works through him. This is quite remarkable, as not only have his dreams of ruling gone unfulfilled but he is now in a far worse state than when he made them. But when he hears that his fellow prisoners have had dreams that trouble them, he tells them that interpretation comes from God and still believes he can help them.

In many ways, these two dreams are less clear than the others. The cupbearer's dream is exceptional only in how mundane it is. Unlike all the other dreams, there is nothing fantastic or unreal about it. The baker's dream is more what we expect a dream to be like, with odd occurrences and a symbolic interpretation. In what amounts to a somewhat macabre pun, Joseph says to both the cupbearer and the baker that Pharaoh will 'lift up [their] head' (vv. 13, 19). Figuratively, the lifted head means 'to treat honourably', but then it is used in a semi-literal sense to refer to the hanging and exposure of the baker.

When Joseph gives the cupbearer his prophecy of restoration, he asks for the cupbearer to plead his case, both on the basis of being innocent of the charge against him, but also as he is the victim of human trafficking. It is somewhat interesting that he refers to himself as 'stolen out of the land of the Hebrews' (v. 15), rather than 'sold by my brothers'; it may suggest that he is attempting to protect the honour of his family. Regardless, his story falls on forgetful ears. While the cupbearer is restored, the text says that he 'did not remember Joseph, but forgot him' (v. 23). Though it is not impossible that the cupbearer is profoundly absent-minded, it is more likely that he finds his position in Pharaoh's service tenuous enough that he does not wish to 'rock the boat' by pleading for the case of a fellow prisoner. If this is so, then for the third time in three stories Joseph finds himself betrayed.

Guidelines

The first several texts in the Joseph cycle can only be described as an ongoing disaster. Family dissolution and oppression of the vulnerable abound, and Joseph in particular seems to be shuffled from one moment of suffering to the next, as he falls from the favoured son of a powerful chieftain to an imprisoned slave.

But one of the problems that many of us have with the reading of these texts is an over-familiarity. We know the story of Joseph. We know it ends well. We know it ends with Joseph in power, saviour of Egypt, saviour and forgiver of his family. It's beautiful – and I mean that legitimately – but our problem is that too often that's all we teach. We miss the horror of these texts. We miss the horror of a man nearly killed and actually trafficked by his brothers. We miss the horror of a slave sexually harassed by his master's wife and then falsely accused of assault. We miss the story of Tamar, thoroughly objectified by man after man, until her best option becomes prostitution.

The story of how God redeems people's pain is beautiful and necessary. But let us never tell that story without acknowledging the reality of the pain and horror and trauma and abuse, the valley of shadow that so many people spend years walking through, waiting and longing for a redemption story.

1 The third set of dreams

Genesis 41:1–24

Genesis 41 is a particularly long narrative, and perhaps the amount of space devoted to this scene reflects its key role in the Joseph cycle. In a series of narratives where nearly everything has gone wrong, especially in Joseph's life, this is the moment when everything starts to turn around. Though he has lost almost everything imaginable, here it begins to be restored. While he doesn't (yet) receive back his family, he receives his freedom, is given a purpose and is placed in a position that will allow his earliest dreams of receiving honour from his family to be realised.

The main scene is of Joseph's audience with Pharaoh, and it begins with another occurrence of the clothing motif that we see elsewhere in the Joseph narratives. When being brought from prison, Joseph shaves and he changes his clothes. While this may simply have been the customary preparation for anyone who was to be brought before Pharaoh, it may also foreshadow the end of Joseph's time as a prisoner.

Upon being introduced as an interpreter of dreams, Joseph says, 'It is not in me; God will give Pharaoh a favourable answer' (v. 16). This is a curious statement, especially given what follows. This statement might be translated, 'God will answer Pharaoh with peace.' Perhaps in an effort to ingratiate himself with Pharaoh, Joseph seems to be suggesting that God will have a good message for Pharaoh.

Perhaps unsurprisingly, Pharaoh's dreams have strong connections to Egyptian life and religious belief. In his dreams, Pharaoh stands at the Nile, and that would seem to be reflective of what is to come. Egypt depends on the flooding of the Nile to keep the soil rich and moist enough to grow crops. Pharaoh is standing on the banks of the river that will fail him. In addition, one of the Egyptian fertility goddesses, Hathor, was sometimes depicted with a cow's head. For Pharaoh to dream of fat cows being devoured by starving cows may have seemed to border on the sacrilegious, and he may have worried that it represented a failure of divine powers. As divine forces were believed to be intimately involved with every aspect of life, it is probable that Pharaoh perceived these disasters as both natural and supernatural. This also suggests that Pharaoh's wise men and diviners are unable to interpret signs that should be familiar to them, but ironically this young foreign man comes immediately and easily to the correct answer.

2 Joseph's plan to save Egypt – and himself

Genesis 41:25–44

In this section, Joseph gives Pharaoh the interpretation of his dream. Both previously in verse 16 and here in verse 25, Joseph tells Pharaoh that God will answer him or that God will reveal his plans. Egyptian belief in the Pharaoh's divinity was quite strong, and so perhaps there is irony here, and even boldness on Joseph's part, at suggesting that his God will answer the individual before him who believes himself to be a god.

Joseph sees the fact that there are two similar dreams as a sign that God is certain about this course and that it will happen soon. But it's a bit odd that he emphasises the double dream here and not elsewhere, especially since the closest parallels to these dreams are his dreams of being given reverence by his family, and they take decades to fulfil and indeed have not yet been fulfilled at this point in the story.

It's also interesting that due to the largely negative interpretation of the dream, Joseph has to revise his earlier statement that God will 'answer Pharaoh with peace', and instead he now simply says, 'God has shown to Pharaoh what he is about to do' (v. 28). In addition to this quick retooling, Joseph segues instantly from dream interpretation to advising. Likely he is attempting to demonstrate that he will be indispensable to the management of the coming crisis, and quite probably trying to avoid being returned to prison. His plans, as recorded in the text, while wise, are not nearly as brilliant as Pharaoh's reaction would suggest. Either we are to read Joseph's words as only a summary of the larger plan that he proposed to Pharaoh, or we are to read Pharaoh's reaction as indicative of God's hand on the direction of Joseph's future and the situation at large.

This interview with Pharaoh concludes in much the same way as it opens, with Joseph again changing dress: this time, to the garments of a powerful Egyptian noble. Perhaps no other individual in scripture has a worldly identity that changes as instantly as this. In less than a day, Joseph moves from a foreign prisoner to the second man in Egypt, so powerful that people are commanded to kneel as he approaches. But soon it will not only be Egyptians who kneel but, as he dreamed long before, his own family.

3 Far from home

Not only does Pharaoh give Joseph a new role and garments, but as part of this overhaul of his identity he gives him a new name. A new identity brought about or confirmed through renaming happens in several places in scripture, such as Abram and Jacob (17:5; 32:28). But on occasion it is the action of a foreign power, probably for the purpose of trying to secure this person in their new identity. Consider Daniel and his friends, whose God-honouring Hebrew names are replaced by Nebuchadnezzar with names that honour Babylonian gods (Daniel 1:7). However, in this story, renaming will also serve to help keep Joseph's true identity concealed from his brothers.

This renaming then lies in contrast to the fact that the now-renamed Joseph gives his sons Hebrew names. The name Manasseh is derived from a rare root that means 'forget', but its few uses suggest that it may indicate an intentional sort of forgetting, perhaps better represented by the English 'forsake'. This would seem to fit with the sense of what Joseph says here, as he has surely not forgotten the actual events, but rather they are not the burden to him that they once were. The name Ephraim is especially interesting. Derived from a root that means 'fruitful', this name suggests once again that God is not a god whose power is limited to Canaan. God has caused Joseph 'to be fruitful and multiply' (1:28). This may also foreshadow the fruitfulness that Israel will experience in Egypt, as they grow from a family to a nation (48:4).

While marrying outside of the family or the nation is typically portrayed negatively (e.g. 26:34–35) and will later be proscribed (Deuteronomy 7:3), there is nothing in the text to imply that Joseph's marriage to an Egyptian should be perceived negatively. And due to this marriage, a large minority of Israel's population had Egyptian ancestry. This might be what lies behind the fascinating laws in Deuteronomy 23:3 that forbid any descendant of a Moabite or an Ammonite from ever entering the assembly of the Lord, but 23:7 allows for the descendants of Edomites and Egyptians to enter the assembly after three generations. While the close relationship with Edom might be understandable, a willingness to include Egyptians is a little harder to understand, until we realise the connection, though a distant one, that exists between Egypt and Israel.

4 A dream fulfilled

Genesis 41:53—42:25

Chapter 41 concludes by preparing us for the next 'act' of the play: Joseph's brothers coming to him for aid. We learn that the famine was not only in Egypt but in 'all the earth' (41:57), but thanks to Joseph's preparations, Egypt becomes the place where people go to buy food. In 42:1, for the first time in four chapters, we return to the story of Jacob and his household. Evidently, Jacob's favouritism is still in play, as he sends all his sons except Benjamin, who is both his youngest and Rachel's only surviving son (as far as he is aware).

When Joseph's brothers arrived in Egypt, we are told that Joseph 'spoke roughly to them'. This is a word that means 'difficult' in many contexts. It seems that Joseph is being intentionally hard on them. Verse 9 says, 'Joseph remembered the dreams that he had dreamed of them.' He sees that this is the moment when those dreams are fulfilled. His brothers are quite literally on their knees before him. The power that he has over them is immense. But rather than abusing his power for the purpose of vengeance, as the chapter progresses we see him 'turn up the heat' to test their character.

Although Joseph at first threatens to take all but one of the brothers hostage until they bring proof of their story in the person of Benjamin, he later decides to hold only one of them. Perhaps this is a matter of compassion, but it may also be that he considers this a better test. One brother would almost certainly return to save all the others, but would the group of men who had once sold one of their number return for the sake of another single brother? He chooses Simeon as hostage, perhaps assuming that he is taking the one most likely to serve as family leader since Reuben's disgrace (35:22). The text states that he 'bound him before their eyes' (42:24), likely as a means of instilling fear.

The brothers immediately suggest that this consequence is a result of their treatment of Joseph years earlier, which causes Joseph to weep, though we are not told why. Does Joseph weep because he thinks his brothers are remorseful and he hopes to be reunited with them? Or does he weep because he hears only resentment in their words and fears that he is no closer to reunion?

5 The return home

Genesis 42:26—43:14

The next piece of Joseph's test isn't entirely revealed until the brothers have returned home. What will the brothers do with this money? Joseph knows that they are greedy. He watched them slaughter the men and plunder the city of Shechem. His murderous brothers decided that selling him was even better than killing him, so that they would not only be rid of Joseph but also be a little richer. But this may be more than a test on Joseph's part: it might also be compassion. He knows that there is a severe famine all over, but he surely has no idea in what sort of financial situation his family finds itself. By returning their money to them, he ensures that they have enough to come and buy food again.

Jacob instructs his sons not only to take restitution for the silver that they found in their bags, but also a gift for the Egyptian noble (Joseph). The gift he suggests is a very generous gift from people who are starving. Medicine and high-calorie, protein-rich foods probably constitute a last-ditch effort to provide for a family who won't make it much longer.

When the brothers first return from Egypt, Jacob's reaction seems to be to write Simeon off as completely as Joseph, despite the fact that there is a clear plan for his restoration (42:36). However, it is interesting that in the discussion that immediately precedes the return to Egypt, Jacob's distress appears to have more to do with the potential risk to Benjamin rather than the actual loss of Simeon (43:6), who is only referred to at the end of the discussion, and then not even by name (43:14). Jacob appears to have reached a point of fatalism, which is perhaps another indication of their desperate situation.

As the brothers negotiate with their father about their return to Egypt and the matter of Benjamin, we begin to see something interesting develop in the personalities and growth of Jacob's sons. Reuben pledges to keep Benjamin safe and promises to give his sons to Jacob to kill if he should fail. The insensitivity of 'here are my two sons to kill' to a man who has already lost two sons and is faced with the potential loss of a third is striking. On the other hand, Judah, a man who has also lost two sons, promises not his living sons, but rather himself as surety.

6 Joseph changes tactics

Genesis 43:15–34

Whereas Joseph was very harsh with his brothers on their first visit, here he connects with his brothers through a surprising extension of kindness and hospitality. When first brought into Joseph's house, the brothers assume that something must be wrong, perhaps connected to the silver placed in their bags. It is interesting that nearly every response of the brothers is a fearful one, perhaps suggesting that they have lived their lives 'looking over their shoulders', waiting for retribution for their treatment of Joseph. But when they try to return the money, Joseph's steward very kindly assures them that payment was received the first time, and the money they found was a gift from God (v. 23).

Far from accusing them of being spies, Joseph invites them to dinner. While hospitality was a high value in the ancient Near East, an Egyptian having a Canaanite to a meal simply didn't happen (v. 32), due to some aspect of the Canaanites that the Egyptians considered 'an abomination'. This word in Hebrew carries a strong sense of not just impropriety but disgust. This would perhaps be the modern equivalent of the Queen inviting up for tea a boy who had been mucking out stables.

In many ways, Joseph is more genuine in this meeting. It could even be a slight slip of his cover that though on the first visit he told his brothers that he thought they were lying, on this occasion he enquires about their father. Once again, Joseph is overcome with emotion, this time upon seeing Benjamin. While it is often emphasised that this is his full brother, and the text bears that out (v. 29), it is not insignificant that this is the brother who did not wrong him.

One further way that he begins to show his hand is by seating them in their birth order (v. 33). Whereas the first meeting between Joseph and his brothers is all about them being 'the other', in this meeting he seems to want them to feel familiar and at home. Verse 34 concludes, 'And they drank and were merry with them,' though this translation obscures the clear Hebrew verb that indicates that they got drunk together. This is a positive ending, and on a literary level it would provide a satisfying outcome: a pleasant dinner that leads to the delightful revelation that their brother is alive. Joseph has one more test, the most severe one yet. But we shall have to wait for a future issue to examine the remainder of these stories.

Guidelines

Without doubt, the church's dialogue about forgiveness is improving, but there is a great deal yet to be said, and I think much benefit could be drawn from the story of Joseph. While we have started to do a good job of explaining that forgiveness, strictly defined, should never enable further mistreatment and does not automatically restore trust or rebuild relationships, we have not yet looked for a path as to how one *does* go about the process of reconciliation. And while the situation between Joseph and his brothers contains too many unique circumstances (not to mention quite a bit of deceit) to create a helpful roadmap, there are some principles that apply. Joseph works through a process. He watches to see how his brothers respond to aggression. He sees how they respond to a clerical error (intentional though it was). He sees how they respond to kindness, and he sees whether they are willing to risk hardship and sacrifice for the good of others.

While I am in no way suggesting that those who have been wronged should attempt to put the one who wronged them through a series of tests, perhaps this shows that reconciliation and restoration might come once it has been determined that real, sustained changes have been made in their life that positively affect how they treat others. Restoration should never be expected, and any reconciliation will be a slow process. But where there is real repentance and good faith, the story of Joseph shows us that it is indeed possible.

FURTHER READING

Joyce G. Baldwin, *The Message of Genesis* (IVP, 1986).
John E. Hartley, *Genesis* (Paternoster Press, 2000).
Gordon Wenham, *Genesis 16–50* (Word, 1994).

Faith under fire: a study of 1 Peter

Gareth Black

1 Peter was originally written to a culturally diverse collective of Christians living out their faith across the Anatolian Peninsula (1:1), united by their suffering. Though their individual grievances vary, they are having a common effect: to raise deeply complex and often destabilising questions vis-à-vis the credibility of their faith and hope in God's promised salvation. It is telling that the first instruction in this letter is to ensure that they think clearly and correctly about the nature of God's salvation (1:3–12) and thereby 'set [stabilise] your hope fully on the grace [of God]' (1:13). Clearly the greatest danger the author perceives in these believers' experiences of suffering is suffering's power to both confuse their thinking and, consequently, subvert their faith in Jesus Christ.

Psychologists have long identified that the devastation of suffering is frequently relative to our expectations. For a Christian who might have mistakenly developed conceptions of God's grace that do not properly account for suffering, facing adversity can be both confusing and even devastating. Relative to their expectations, such experiences might suggest that either Christianity is bogus or, if it is legitimate, their circumstances indicate that they personally have become disqualified. It is this incoherent tension between one's (misplaced) expectations of the nature of God's grace and a lived experience of suffering that harbours the power to unhinge Christian faith and hope, a struggle that the apostle Peter experienced all too personally (Matthew 16:21–28; Mark 8:31–38).

If misunderstanding of God's grace, however sincerely held, facilitates fertile soil for suffering's undermining of faith, one solution is surely to offer believers a *true* account of how that grace does – and doesn't – operate in salvation, one that fully accounts for experiences of suffering and endows them with meaning. 5:12 clearly reveals this to be the purpose of 1 Peter. Its author wrote with a clear intention: to present what is *true* about the nature of God's grace in salvation, so that we might become fully convinced that we can 'stand firm' upon it in navigating life and faith's many trials.

Unless otherwise stated, Bible quotations are taken from the ESV.

1   Salvation that is suffering-secure

1 Peter 1:1–13

Given the purpose highlighted in the introduction to these notes, it makes perfect sense that the letter opens with an invigorating summary articulating what is true about the grandeur, purview and security of God's salvation syllabus.

Verses 3–12 are structured according to three temporal dimensions of God's salvation. There is a *future* reality to salvation (vv. 3–5) in which the hope of their promised inheritance cannot be undermined by the circumstances of this world, because it exists beyond this world, 'kept in heaven for you' (v. 4) and is exclusively contingent upon the unchangeable historical reality of Jesus' resurrection (v. 3). There is also a *past* component (vv. 9–12) in which Israel's ancient prophets, who themselves faced the challenge of believing in Christ without the luxury of physically seeing him (compare vv. 8–9), had predicted that 'the sufferings of Christ and the subsequent glories' (v. 11) would be the means through which God would elect to provide salvation. There is also a *present* dynamic to Christian salvation (vv. 6–9) in which, 'if necessary' (v. 6), God is able to use grievous and testing experiences to refine our faith, so that even though, like any tested metal, it might appear to emerge from the fire smaller, it does so purer and, therefore, of greater value.

When our thinking is recalibrated, it offers us a perspective on what is true about the grace of God (5:12) that both stabilises our basis for hope and endows experiences of suffering with serious purpose and meaning. As Israel literally *girded up their loins* in Egypt to enable them to journey effectively towards their promised inheritance in Canaan, verse 13 suggests that Christian success in walking towards our inheritance is to prepare our minds (literally, 'gird up the loins of your mind') with this true understanding of God's salvation. Only with our minds clear and focused upon these realities can we stand secure against the challenges and pressures of our present wilderness journey.

2 God's provision of a salvation thought-model

1 Peter 1:13—2:10

What might be the significance of this letter describing its mostly Gentile audience in terms such as 'exiles' chosen 'for obedience to Jesus Christ and for sprinkling with his blood' (1:1–2), or as 'ransomed… with the precious blood of Christ, like that of a lamb without blemish or spot' (1:18–19), or 'living stones… being build up as a spiritual house' (2:5), or, indeed, 'a chosen race, a royal priesthood, a holy nation, a people for his own possession' (2:9)?

Clearly these metaphors are drawn very intentionally from the book of Exodus, through which Peter intends his readers to capture important aspects of their own salvation. The aptness of pointing people to this story is profound: Exodus was *itself* a salvation journey, one that began with Israel being 'called out of the darkness' in Egypt to live in God's light as 'a people for his own possession' (2:9) until the realisation of their promised inheritance (1:4) in Canaan. It was a salvation curriculum that, by God's design, included ransoming at the price of the unblemished Passover lamb (1:19), discoveries of God's holiness and their covenantal commitment to obey God's moral law (1:15–16), an act symbolically sealed by Moses sprinkling blood upon the people (1:2). It involved the founding of Israel into a chosen race and nation (2:9–10), as well as the establishment of a spiritual house (tabernacle) with its attending priesthood and system of worship (2:5) designed specifically to proclaim for both the Israelites and surrounding nations the 'excellencies' of God's wisdom and mercy (2:9).

Hebrews 8:5, however, tells us that the ultimate purpose of all the dynamics of Israel's salvation journey was to 'serve [as] a copy and shadow of heavenly things'. In other words, in the same way that scientists create molecular models in order to help them understand aspects of organic chemistry, God has offered the world a historic model of his salvation in Israel's Exodus by which we may capture many of the dynamics and realities of his grace and processes in Christian salvation. What a resource this must have been to the first recipients of 1 Peter, in the absence of the New Testament canon to help them understand these things. Rather than Peter needing to explain the dynamics of God's salvation grace in abstractions, God provided an accessible thought-model in Israel's Exodus experience through which to discover – or rediscover - crucial realities about the nature of our salvation in Christ.

3 Suffering *in spite of* doing good

1 Peter 2:11–25

A major part of God's plan for Israel's salvation in Exodus was to include a liminal period – between exiting Egypt and inheriting Canaan – of learning to sojourn in the wilderness as exiles. Despite Israel's early enthusiasm and devotion to God, the monotony and challenges of their wilderness experience became a crucible that tested the genuineness of their faith in God (compare Deuteronomy 8). It revealed that many of them did not trust God at all. Drawing from Exodus, 1 Peter encourages Christians to understand their present, liminal period – between being 'born again' (1:3) and receiving our promised inheritance (1:4) at Jesus' revelation (1:5, 13) – as that of 'exiles' (1:1; v. 11), where our faith can expect similar pressures to that of Israel's wilderness wanderings.

Of course, inherent to being a Christian exile is a sense of alienation, as well as questions of how to navigate the tensions that can arise from living alongside those who do not share our worldview or values. At one level, these challenges are *internal*, in terms of how we resist the powerful 'passions of the flesh' (v. 11). At another level, the challenges are *external* and relational, in terms of how we as Christians conduct our public lives and positively interact with others who do not presently believe the gospel, say, in contexts of civic governance (vv. 13–17), employment and service (vv. 18–25) or even marriage (3:1–7). 1 Peter emphasises that Christians bear responsibility before God for conducting themselves in these environments with respect and positive engagement, not because people will always merit it (sometimes they definitely won't!), but rather because doing so accords with God's grace and will that we have been called to (vv. 19–21). It is also central to the integrity and effectiveness of Christian public witness (v. 12).

That is not to say that doing so will be easy! 1 Peter is very honest that, at times, despite our best efforts we may suffer unjustly *in spite of* all the good we do (v. 18). Nevertheless, our response to these challenges is to be determined by the gospel and not by the level of injustice we may have experienced, nor by simply demanding our rights. Given how countercultural and counterintuitive that kind of response is in our current social milieu, 1 Peter points us to another model to inspire us: Jesus Christ, who did not fight fire with fire when unjustly suffering, but steadfastly entrusted himself to the promise of true justice whilst continuing to do good (v. 23).

4 Suffering *because of* doing good

1 Peter 3:8–22

1 Peter never sentimentalises the nature of God's grace in our salvation, but instead makes repeatedly clear that God's bringing us to glory often involves suffering; it certainly did for Jesus (1:11; 2:20–25), and it may for us. We have already seen that one way a Christian might face adversity is by suffering unjustly, *in spite of* doing good (2:18–25). Today's passage focuses on another form of grief: suffering 'for righteousness' sake' (v. 14) – pain and opposition we face directly *because of* our 'doing good' (v. 17).

Often 'doing good' does not cause us to suffer. Quite the opposite: verses 8–13 suggests that we ought to do good in the form of guarding our speech and not reciprocating animosity because there is both a divine blessing (v. 9) and a strong correlation between being the kind of person who is keen to always 'do good' or 'seek peace' (v. 11) and experiencing a pleasant life. However, 1 Peter is realistic enough to recognise that there may come occasions where we are made to suffer precisely *because* we have done what is right (vv. 14, 17), for example, when someone loses friendships because they courageously confront misogynistic behaviour, or when an individual's career progression is curtailed because they refuse to cut ethical corners in business for the sake of higher profit margins. 1 Peter's expectation is that, as Christians, we need to be prepared to face suffering of this type.

We are to do so, however, in a particular way: by not allowing these challenges to unnerve us (v. 14b); by making clear that our supreme loyalty is to Christ as Lord (v. 15); and by displaying to others that the Christian 'hope within you' is a hope that transcends even the ideals of personal safety, material wealth or social reputation. This reiterates a key message of 1 Peter, namely, that how we as Christians respond to suffering is a crucial factor in our public witness, with huge evangelistic potential in commending Christ to others. The assumption in verse 15 is that, as we suffer faithfully, it will provoke curiosity among others regarding the basis for the intriguing hope they observe in us. This raises two sobering questions: if we never receive questions about our faith, just how much is the distinctive power and hope of Christianity on display in our lives? And, when those questions do come, how capable and prepared are we to graciously offer meaningful and persuasive answers concerning the rational and evidential basis for Christianity's claims?

5 Suffering *because of* the name of Christ

We will focus on verses 12–19, where 1 Peter addresses a final form of suffering that a Christian may face: suffering 'as a Christian' (v. 16) or 'for the name of Christ' (v. 14). Unlike the previous forms of grief considered, which are neither unique to Christians nor determined by allegiance to Christ per se, the 'fiery trial' (v. 12) considered here concerns adversity caused directly because of one's Christian faith.

Verse 12 emphasises a message implied throughout the letter: when these experiences of suffering emerge, we ought not to be 'surprised', as if such things are incoherent abnormalities in God's grace that in some way discredit his salvation promise. This was precisely why Peter was so unnerved by Jesus' pronouncement of his sufferings and rejection (compare Mark 8:31–38); he simply had no category for the hope of salvation he had entrusted to Jesus containing such difficulties. Yet Jesus was very intentional in forewarning his followers about the opposition that would come both to himself and to his disciples (compare John 15:18–25). He did so in order that when these experiences inevitably came, rather than undermine their faith in his words, sending them into all kinds of spiritual confusion, it would *confirm* their trust in him. Instead of being unsettled by these experiences of suffering, we are to 'rejoice' (v. 13); not rejoice masochistically in the experience of suffering, but rejoice in what it means: we 'share Christ's sufferings'; we share in being insulted and rejected on the same basis that Christ did. Though we might experience disassociation from others because of our allegiance to Christ, in such moments God associates with us with profound levels of intimacy; the very 'spirit of glory and of God' rests upon us (v. 14). And, if we share in Christ's sufferings, we will also share in his glory and vindication, on the day when Christ is revealed as Lord and those who have faithfully followed Jesus are declared by history's true judge to have been on the right side of history (v. 14; 5:1).

Though all experiences of Christian persecution are acutely difficult, we must not be ashamed (v. 16; Mark 8:38), but instead 'entrust [our] souls to a faithful Creator while doing good' (v. 19), assured that God can use even the fire of adversity to both reveal what is true ('judge') about the quality of our faith (vv. 17–18), and refine that faith into something so valuable that it will receive the very commendation of heaven itself (1:6–7).

6 Suffering and shepherding

What qualities do you expect in a Christian leader? Commanding presence? Charismatic personality? Inspirational visionary? As typical as these attributes are to our notions – even Christian notions – of good leadership, they are not the primary qualities that 1 Peter advocates for spiritual oversight. Instead, and unsurprisingly given the purpose of the letter, the charge is laid for leaders ('elders', v. 1) to demonstrate qualities that will ultimately enable those in their care to suffer well and stand firm in Christian hope when their faith is under fire.

Verses 1–4, however, highlight that this crucial component of leadership ought to be augmented by both the example that leaders personally set in navigating faith under fire (v. 3b) and by the character with which leaders lead others (vv. 2–3). Much of what Peter himself learned about walking through pain and suffering with hope intact was grasped 'as a witness of the sufferings of Christ' (v. 1). He observed first-hand Jesus' example par excellence of what it meant to respond to adversity and injustice by 'entrust[ing] his soul to a faithful Creator while doing good' (4:19). Do we as leaders appreciate the value of our own example in helping others navigate disappointment, illness, injustice, even death in a truly Christian way?

The character with which leaders lead is also crucial. Devastating spiritual damage can be done when influential leaders abuse their power by treating people in manipulative or 'domineering' ways (v. 3) or exploit Christian ministry for 'shameful gain' (v. 2), or perhaps are persistently negative about their experience of leadership in a plea for self-pity. Instead, Christian leaders are to 'shepherd the flock of God that is among you' (v. 2). Suffering, present or future, raises all kinds of challenges for Christian character and faith. In such crucibles, people don't need a champion-leader who appears invulnerable to the demands of the struggle; neither do we need a general-leader who will ride roughshod over people's fears and weaknesses. We need a shepherd; someone who knows the terrain, appreciates the perils, is patient with weaknesses, does not abandon lost sheep and will gently, resolutely and faithfully serve to lead the weary safely home.

Guidelines

I wonder if you have been struck by the realism of this letter's understanding of the challenges that suffering brings to both our personal psychology and our faith in God's promised salvation through Christ. How we interpret and respond to experiences of suffering will be influenced by a variety of factors. It can be easy, when not suffering, to confidently and in all sincerity assert various abstract theological platitudes. Yet the actual experience of walking through pain and suffering can shake our faith and make those platitudes appear desperately insufficient. This is why studying scripture to learn the nature of God's grace is not simply an abstract theological exercise, but of vital pastoral significance to our own faith and that of those we might lead.

- What are the questions and dilemmas that suffering raises for me? Am I confident that God takes these questions seriously, or is there a suspicion that God will be disappointed with me for questioning my faith?

- What are my expectations of God in relation to pain and suffering? Do I feel that an all-powerful God who loves me shouldn't allow disappointment or injustice? Do I expect God to answer my prayer and intervene to change my circumstances? What if that doesn't happen, or heaven appears silent?

- 1 Peter refers to the 'sufferings' of Christ as our example in navigating adversity faithfully. As familiar as I might be with the gospels, have I ever taken time to 'be a witness of the sufferings of Christ' (5:1), studying how Jesus responded to pain and opposition so that I may learn from it?

- To know you are not alone in your suffering can be profoundly helpful (1 Peter 5:9). In what ways can I draw encouragement and inspiration from the stories of other Christians who have walked through valleys of pain – either in history or presently in various parts of the world – so that I can learn and find support in managing my own experiences of pain? How might I break taboos and facilitate conversations on issues with other Christians?

FURTHER READING

David Gooding, *Peter: Scholar and teacher in the school of suffering* (Myrtlefield House, 2017). Available online: **myrtlefieldhouse.com/en/resource/493/peter-scholar-and-teacher-in**

Karen H. Jobes, *1 Peter* (Baker Academic, 2005).

C.S. Lewis, *A Grief Observed* (Faber, 1966).

Exodus 1—24

Richard Briggs

Welcome to the greatest sequel ever told – in which the (Egyptian) empire strikes back...

If Genesis is the extraordinary widescreen visionary opening of holy scripture, then Exodus is where the story gets political. Here we find slavery and escape; conflict and confrontation; powerful signs and hardened hearts – all leading up to the fly-by-night exodus that takes the Israelites through the mysteriously parted sea and out into the possibilities (and the terrors) of the wilderness beyond.

There are several ways to focus our engagement with the story. First, we have the figure of Moses, Israel's emergent and reluctant national leader – a man thrust into the heart of Pharaoh's court and into the pressures of leadership. Second, there is the showdown between the God of Israel and the gods of Egypt, matching each other miracle for miracle as the battle builds towards its intense Passover resolution. Third comes the journey – the 'exodus' itself – across the sea and towards the land to which God is calling them. For all the exultation of escape, in the praise of the 'Song of the Sea' in chapter 15 especially, the realities of wilderness wandering will prove testing.

Then, most mysterious of all, comes the realisation that freedom from Egypt leads Israel out to Mount Sinai where they meet with God and receive... the law. This is key: freedom from slavery to Egypt leads not to 'freedom' from being subject to requirements, but rather leads to being God's servants. Perhaps this is Exodus in one sentence: Israel (God's people) is transferred from Pharaoh's ownership to God's ownership. The 'freedom' is freedom to serve God, and the book of Exodus intends to show that this is life-giving service, rather than the slavery of serving the empire.

Unless otherwise stated, Bible quotations are taken from the NRSV.

1 How revolutions begin: the midwives' story

Exodus 1

After the briefest of recaps of Jacob's family coming to Egypt (verses 1–7 reprise Genesis 46:8–27), the narrator jumps straight in to engaging with the 'enemy'. Egypt's 'new king' (v. 8, more commonly known as Pharaoh) is described solely in terms of not knowing Joseph, which was probably not top of his own version of his CV. He builds store cities and makes the Israelites' lives hard. The word for 'store cities' (*miskenot*) would have made a striking contrast with God's dwelling – later in the book – in the tabernacle (the *mishkan*), and also a striking contrast with Israel's later reliance on daily manna in the desert. The portrait of Egypt as the ancient equivalent of a ruthless and industrialised nation starts here.

The narrative really takes off, though, with Pharaoh's gruesome decision to have any Hebrew boys killed at birth. Note that he will let the girls live, based presumably on his estimation that it is the men who will cause him trouble, not the women. But reflect for a moment on how this chapter (and indeed the next one) plays out: who causes all the trouble for Pharaoh here? It is the women. And even if that were not true, clearly Pharaoh is making a decision here that will reduce or even remove his stock of male Israelite slaves, thus undermining his whole programme of forced labour. Thus far he has been wrong about everything.

The women of 1:15 are literally 'the midwives of/from the Hebrews' – which could mean they were Hebrew midwives, or (Gentile) midwives to the Hebrews. Either way, we are told they 'feared God' (v. 17), rather than that they were simply being loyal Israelites. This sense of 'fearing God' is fundamentally about deep respect, or sometimes reverence, out of which comes their remarkable decision to lie to Pharaoh. Civil disobedience comes hot on the heels of oppressive power. As Martin Luther King would have said: civil rights start here.

Verse 20 is unequivocal: God is on the side of the midwives. Although Pharaoh's immediate response is to reinforce the death-wish – and like most uprisings things are going to get worse before they get better – it is not stretching matters to say that the revolution begins in the hearts of two midwives. Let kings with ears to hear, hear.

2 The women and the water (and the well)

Exodus 2

More stories of women causing trouble for Pharaoh. None of them are named here, although we will later learn that one of them is Miriam, and we will eventually learn names for Moses' parents, but all the names are held back in this story to help emphasise verse 10: 'She named him Moses.' Here, the name Moses is linked to the Hebrew verb *mashah*, 'to draw out'. Well, that's the narrator's story. Egyptians probably thought it came from 'born of', as in Egyptian names like 'Ramases' ('born of Ra' – the sun God). Even on details like this, Israel's scriptures are telling a different story to the perspective of the empire.

The woman desperately hiding her baby (v. 3) puts him in a *tebah*. The word is used only here and in Genesis 6—9, where it refers to the ark. In each case, this is salvation from the water in a container that preserves a life for God. This is the first of many details in Exodus that highlights this book as a kind of second Genesis: the creation of the nation of Israel rather than of the whole world.

Pharaoh's daughter finds and loves the baby, and ends up paying the birth-mother to nurse him, thus funding another breaking of Pharaoh's law. He is still not as in-charge as he thinks he is.

There follows a brief interlude featuring no women (vv. 11–15). Instead, it features what we might describe as murder, cover-up and running away. Was the murder a righteous act of defiance? The narrative does not say. If a character's opening story serves as their character note, this is not a great beginning for Moses, miraculously saved from death and then raised in the royal court. He is going to have to relearn his own identity before he can take on his calling.

First, in Midian, he meets a woman at a well. This has happened before (Genesis 24, 29) and it will happen again (John 4). Wells were the water-coolers around which love could be found (which Jesus is redefining in that final example). Sure enough, Moses ends up with a Midianite wife and a son called 'Gershom' ('a stranger there'). The stage is almost set.

Then the Israelites cry out, and God 'hears... remembers... looks... and sees'. Now the stage is set.

3 The great 'I AM'

A burning bush draws Moses off the beaten track – though, let's be honest, there was no beaten track out in the wilderness. As the KJV once put it, Moses has now come 'to the backside of the desert'. Far removed from the centres of power, indeed from anything, he encounters God.

We should be clear here. Horeb is 'the mountain of God' (and the ground is 'holy') because God is there. This was not otherwise a holy site: it was a bush, in the desert. But because God was there it became holy, requiring Moses to tread carefully. (In fact, Horeb will turn out to be Sinai, and Moses will be back on this mountain later for the ten commandments.)

The bush burns but never burns up. The word for 'bush' (*sineh*) sounded like the word 'Sinai', and in a story where never a word is wasted, this called to mind a striking image. Israel may experience life with God as being like a burning fire – overwhelming and often disorientating – and yet the picture of the bush tells them, up front, that they will never be consumed by the fire.

In meeting this God of holiness, Moses is commissioned to be the one who will help God deal with the oppression noted at the end of chapter 2 (see vv. 9–10). It becomes rapidly clear that Moses is a lot less excited about being chosen for this task than one might have expected, and his ongoing dialogue on the matter will occupy us through much of chapter 4. Here our focus is on the God who meets him in this fiery encounter.

Moses wants to know who this God is. Verse 6 has already given one answer – the God of the great forefathers of the faith (Abraham, Isaac and Jacob). But in verse 14 we reach the ultimate answer: 'I AM WHO I AM.' English Bibles print this in capital letters to mark it as the name of God, based in turn on a form of the verb 'to be'. (Scholars suggest it may have been the word 'Yahweh', traditionally rendered over the centuries as 'Jehovah', and known only by its consonants Y-H-W-H.) In short: God is the one who is. Always. So no fire, or Pharaoh, will stand against him.

4 'Send someone else'

The focus switches to Moses' repeated attempts to get out of his calling. Five times he tries to put a problem in the way, starting back in 3:11 with 'Who am I that I should go…?' (which is interestingly close to the wording at stake in God's self-identification in response as 'I AM'). Then, following through the narrative: 'Who are you?' (3:13); 'What if they do not believe me?' (v. 1); 'I am slow of speech' (v. 10); and finally, perhaps desperately, and out of excuses, 'Please send someone else' (v. 13).

God deals patiently with all these excuses, at least until the last one. The third objection is met with power to do all that the Egyptian magicians can do – not because that is a good thing in itself, but simply to speed Moses on his way to the encounter. The fourth objection is usually understood as suggesting that Moses had some kind of speech impediment. This then gets addressed after the fifth and final (and weakest) complaint, where God is at last angry, and says he will send Moses' brother Aaron with him. This is Aaron's first mention in the Bible, put forward as an eloquent accomplice for all that is to follow. Interestingly, at no point in the subsequent story does Aaron play this role for Moses. Maybe the issue in this dialogue with God is all about Moses' sense of inadequacy and not the reality of what will happen when he does move ahead.

In a nice touch, foreshadowing what is to come, Moses goes to his father-in-law and says, 'Please let me go…' and Jethro replies 'Go in peace' (v. 18). If only it would prove this simple to take his leave when he comes to ask Pharaoh to let them go. Verses 21–23 more or less spell out that it will not be like that.

Then God meets Moses on the road and tries to kill him. A strong candidate for one of the most obscure mini-narratives in all of scripture, verses 24–26 seems to have Zipporah save Moses with a bloodied foreskin touched to his 'feet' (which sometimes stands as a euphemism for 'genitals'). Is this about circumcision, in some way? The effect – like with Jacob wrestling the angel – is to confront Moses with the danger and difficulty of the task ahead. More than that, who knows?

5 Bricks without straw

'Let my people go' is Moses and Aaron's opening gambit, as the showdown with Pharaoh finally gets underway (v. 1) – and is derailed immediately.

'Who is the Lord?' asks Pharaoh. Now where have we seen this pattern before? A hard word from Pharaoh – a creative version of the truth in response (Moses and Aaron are planning a full-scale departure, not just a three-day worship meeting) – and then a ramping up of the harshness of Pharaoh's demands… this is a repeat of the midwives' situation back in chapter 1. Moses and Aaron's account in verse 3, based as it is on what God said the elders could say to Pharaoh back in 3:18, may not be an actual lie, but is certainly not the whole truth, nor the point of their engagement with Pharaoh.

Pharaoh's response, which we will come to in a moment, certainly makes things worse. The Israelites are unimpressed, unsurprisingly, and are blunt with Moses and Aaron: 'You have brought us into bad odour with Pharaoh' (v. 21) – better captured by the ESV's 'You have made us stink in the sight of Pharaoh'. Any last illusions that this would go smoothly are destroyed.

But note that what is presented by Moses and Aaron as a matter of worship is heard immediately by Pharaoh as a matter of economics (see v. 8). It is the three days' loss of labour (and income) that enrages him. Hence the once-again self-defeating fury: let them make bricks without straw (which is hardly going to improve or speed up his building projects). The bricks were probably wet clay and straw, baked in the sun – and the phrasing of 'baking bricks' in verse 7 echoes the language used in describing the building of the tower of Babel in Genesis 11:3. This is forced labour in pursuit of self-aggrandisement, without regard to what would even make sense in building terms. The result is a workforce tiring themselves out looking for 'stubble' (v. 12) and failing to make their quotas.

The gods of Egypt do not include one known as 'economic expansionism' – but in effect that is the picture painted in this opening section of Exodus. Is there any chance that worship and faithfulness can defeat the well-heeled empire? Were we paying attention when the story started out with the midwives and their local acts of defiance? Is the world any different today?

6 'I will be your God'

In some ways Exodus 6 is a taking stock – repeating some of the core elements of the story so far. God reveals himself magisterially to Moses, identifying himself by his name 'Y-H-W-H', as in chapter 3. God commissions Moses to go and confront Pharaoh, and Moses complains that he is a 'poor speaker' (v. 12, repeated in v. 30), as in chapter 4. Still God sends Moses, albeit along with Aaron, to play the part God has prepared for them (v. 13, 26), as again in chapter 4. And some sense of Moses' backstory is also included, though very differently. Where chapter 2 told stories about how he came to be part of his birth and adopted families, here verses 14–25 give us just enough of Israel's genealogy to locate Moses and his brother in their family line. Chapter 6 ends where it began – anticipating the showdown that the bricks-without-straw debacle had set up in chapter 5. So what is going on?

Biblical scholars often get waylaid at this point by theories about where the book of Exodus came from, and they suggest that much of chapter 6 is effectively an alternate version of what we have read already: the story as told by someone else. But the more interesting question is what effect this kind of step back and reviewing of issues creates as we read through the book. We have reached the very beginning of the plagues narrative and are about to enter into the full-on conflict between Moses et al and Pharaoh. How did it come to this? Was there no other way? Chapter 6 is like a calm-before-the-storm recap of the story, to indicate that this was what had to happen. There was no other way the story of God, Israel, Egypt, Moses and the slaves and Pharaoh would ever have ended.

The God in question is magnificently described in verses 2–8. Not just 'I AM', but El Shaddai (which probably connoted power or strength); committed to Israel by covenant and compassion; determined to act by his mighty hand, or his outstretched arm, and to free them from burdens. This is who God really is, and one of the many indictments of the cruelty of Israel's slavery is that they are too broken to see it (v. 9).

So of course Moses has to go, and confrontation has to follow. Exodus 6 confirms how much is at stake.

Guidelines

There is a brief moment in Exodus 2 when, happily married and tending his father-in-law's flocks, Moses is able to catch a glimpse of a quiet life. As he makes his way over to examine the burning bush, perhaps he even contemplates adopting a little desert mysticism. Good job, good family, with time to encounter God in prayer – what more could a man want?

It is not to be. Exodus is not a book of peace or prosperity. In fact, it is deeply suspicious of prosperity, which it portrays as achieved by the blood and sweat of badly treated slaves, and it is under no illusions about peace. If the powers of Egypt have their way, the God of Israel will be marginalised – mocked as a nobody (as in 5:2).

But behold the two great passages of divine self-revelation, in chapters 3 and 6: the God of Israel is the God who (always) 'is', acting from the compassion of seeing what has happened to his people.

The book of Exodus sets before us a remarkable picture of a conflict of powers. Against the might of the Egyptian power comes a small band of inelegant and ineloquent slaves – they will be described variously as a 'mixed crowd' and a 'rabble' at various points in the Pentateuch, and yet their determination to be allowed to worship their God triggers a conflict that will bring down Pharaoh. The odds are all against them, but that seems to be how God often chooses to work in the Old Testament.

The 21st-century world is just as fixated on making its own versions of bricks without straw, without reference to the human misery involved. Whether we are called to be a Moses, a midwife, a Miriam down by the river or a member of the workforce, we fight the same fight today, for the same God.

18–24 July

1 The ten plagues

Exodus 7:1–24; 11:1–8

Today we read about the first and last of the plagues. Chapters 7—11 give us ten: water turned to blood; frogs; gnats; flies; death of livestock; boils; hail; locusts; darkness; and the death of the firstborn. This is not a PG-rated section of scripture, *Prince of Egypt* notwithstanding.

Exodus 7 sets the story in motion by way of a quick resumé of the story so far, including the startling 7:1, where God says to Moses 'I have made you like God to Pharaoh' – accurately rendered in the ever-literal KJV as 'I have made thee a God to Pharaoh'. The 'like' is added to avoid misunderstanding, but in effect the text says Moses now plays God to Pharaoh, who will play the role of the Egyptian God. The showdown is intense: sometimes the Egyptian magicians can match Moses (plague one – 7:22) and sometimes they cannot (plague three – 8:18). Is it that a sign on its own may or may not be enough?

One underlying issue is getting Egypt/Pharaoh to recognise that it is the Lord who is God. This is the purpose of the power display – see 7:5 and also 9:14–16, which serves as a reflection as plague seven gets underway, touching on both the purpose of all this and also why it is taking so long.

If you read through all of Exodus 7—11, it is a dark and terrifying series of narratives, seemingly without end. Respite is rare (8:15 and 9:34 are isolated moments). There is no straightforward progression in intensity, but the penultimate plague – dense darkness for three days – foreshadows the final deathly episode.

Plague ten is threatened in chapter 11, and promised to be climactic: 'every firstborn in the land of Egypt shall die' (11:5) – from Pharaoh to the slaves to the livestock. This is presented as retribution for what Egypt has done to Israel: compare Pharaoh's killing of Hebrew children back in 1:22 or the Lord's explanation to Moses in 4:22–23, which seems to anticipate this turn of events. Unexpectedly, the Israelites are to take the Egyptians' gold and silver with them when they leave. In due course, this will resource the building of both the tabernacle and the golden calf: a hint that the exodus itself is not the simple 'happy end' of the story.

2 Pharaoh's hardened heart

Exodus 10

We loop back, out of order, to pick up a key issue that runs throughout the plague narratives, concerning the hardening of Pharaoh's heart. Chapter 10 offers a sample reading that picks out some of the examples of this repeated point. It is actually the narrative of plague eight (locusts, vv. 1–20) and plague nine (darkness, vv. 21–20).

What we observe here is the culmination of a gradual intensifying of the notes about Pharaoh's hard heart, whereby each of the first nine plagues concludes with a reference of some kind to it. Here we have a clear statement in verse 20 that plague eight ends with the Lord hardening Pharaoh's heart, and then likewise with plague nine in verse 27 – as Moses starts to ask for more than just permission to leave, adding in demands for livestock after Pharaoh seems to have conceded in verse 24. The whole chapter is prefaced with the Lord telling Moses that this is what he will do (v. 1). So what is going on?

First, what does it mean? The 'heart' in Hebrew was where the thinking took place. There could be an emotional element, but the focus was on understanding. Some new translations depart therefore from the Hebrew wording and suggest 'the Lord made Pharaoh stubborn' (e.g. CEB). The idea – quite literally – is that he cannot see reason.

Second, careful readers have long noted an interesting progression in the phrasing used, whereby the first five plague narratives have Pharaoh be the agent of his hardened heart – i.e. either he hardens his own heart (8:15; 8:32) or his heart 'remains' or 'was' hardened (7:22; 8:19; 9:7). Plague six introduces God hardening Pharaoh's heart (9:12), which is what we see here in chapter 10 again. And recall that this means something like 'Pharaoh refused to see reason' / 'God made Pharaoh unable to see reason'.

The idea seems to be that God takes up Pharaoh's own stubbornness and effectively hands him over to it – come the midpoint of the plagues narrative, it is no longer possible for Pharaoh to have second thoughts, because his chance to act rightly has gone. Human freedom and divine action, as so often in the Old Testament, are understood as working together, not in tension. But note too: God did see this coming (see 4:21; 7:3).

3 The first Passover

Exodus 12:1–36

Verses 1–28 indicate the preparations for the exodus: instructions for what becomes the first Passover. It is a meal eaten 'with their boots on', as we might paraphrase verse 11. Its name is simple and descriptive: a 'pass-over' (v. 11) because the Lord will 'pass over you' (v. 13). The Hebrew name (*Pesach*) actually means 'protection', highlighting that in passing over the houses, those with blood on the doorframe are protected – a detail absent from chapter 11's announcement of this final plague, though possibly linking back to that strange story in 4:24–26.

All this is so significant that the calendar is reset to mark the start of the year here (v. 2). This falls around March/April in modern terms, although alternative Jewish traditions still celebrate their new year in the autumn, at the time of the harvest. Exodus thus imagines Passover as more significant and more life-giving than the annual harvest.

Part of the chapter is about setting up Passover as an annual memorial (vv. 14, 24–27). Note the emphasis on teaching its significance to children, which, like the meal of lamb (v. 3) and the unleavened bread (v. 39), remains at the heart of Jewish Passover celebration. In many languages the word derived from *Pesach* is also the name of Easter, since Christ's death and resurrection took place at Passover. In their different ways, Jews and Christians both celebrate here the triumph of life over death – or as Exodus puts it, summing up the conflict between the Israelite and the Egyptian powers, God says 'on all the gods of Egypt I will execute judgements' (v. 12).

Verse 28 pivots back to the overall setting: Israel prepares obediently. And then the narrative unfolds at speed: at midnight, the Lord strikes; plague ten arrives in full force; Pharaoh realises all is lost, and too late he sends Moses, Aaron and the people to 'go, worship the Lord, as you said' (v. 31). At the last moment the oppressor even asks the oppressed for a blessing (v. 32), but perhaps Exodus suggests by its silence here that Pharaoh has finally and fully reaped what he has sown.

But if Israel's suffering is dealt with, they do not yet have new life in all its fullness. For that, one more resurrection-shaped and life-giving miracle will be needed as they flee.

4 The exodus: God's new creation

Exodus 13:17—14:31

After some rules about future celebration of all these momentous events, 13:17 takes us back to the exodus itself. It tells us that they did not take the coastal route ('the way of… the Philistines') – even though that was quicker – but they took a more circuitous wilderness path. Where they went exactly has puzzled commentators ever since, but in due course it loops south down through the Sinai peninsula, which they are traversing from the west (Egypt) to the north-east (the land of Canaan). At some point, they end up far enough south to hit the 'Red Sea', as the ancient Greek and Latin translations had it in 13:18, as a result of which most English Bibles say the same. It is well known that the Hebrew phrase is actually 'sea of reeds', which is unlikely to mean the (salty, reed-free) Red Sea. In whatever way, think of it as 'the sea at the end of the world': threatening enough to die in if pursued into it by Pharaoh's chariots.

And here they come, following furiously (14:5–6), and with Pharaoh as stubborn as ever once again – 'heart hardened'. Is the conflict still not over?

Two of the many features of this 'exodus' narrative stand out. One is that now the Lord is directly engaged in delivering Israel, and the conflict is indeed (therefore) over. Note that 14:14 tells Israel they only have to keep still (because the Lord will fight for them), and then 14:15 says 'tell [them] to go forward'! God has this in hand – indeed, in Moses' hand (14:16).

Then note also how God's 'wind' blows to separate the waters of the sea and to create dry land (v. 21). The word for 'wind' (*ruach*) elsewhere means 'spirit' – and this image reminds us of Genesis 1, where God's *ruach* hovered over the waters and dry land was created. (The 'dry land' of Exodus 14:16, 22, 29 is the same word as Genesis 1:9). Israel is delivered to new life by this 'new creation' story. We might almost say: the exodus is creation-time for the nation of Israel. Or more generally: creation and salvation are two sides of the same story.

5   The song of the sea

Exodus 15:1–21

The extraordinary events of Exodus 14 are here taken up in song – two songs to be precise, one sung by Moses and the Israelites (vv. 1–18) and one sung by Miriam and all the women (vv. 20–21). Maybe Miriam led the company in the whole of Moses' song, since verse 21 is a kind of reprise of verse 1 – is it short-hand for saying that all the women joined in praise? That clearly happened in Israel on other occasions (e.g. 1 Samuel 18:6–7).

The resulting burst of praise is known in Hebrew tradition as 'the song of the sea' and is a poetic retelling of the story we have just read, and more. It is one of very few passages traditionally written or printed as a poem – i.e. with a lot of blank space around its words on the scroll. This emphasises how special the text is, since scrolls were expensive and usually every inch was covered.

The theme of the song is that the Lord has won a great victory at the crossing of the sea, throwing Pharaoh and his army into the waters. Verse 12 says 'the earth swallowed them', which is poetic license for the sea actually swallowing them. The Lord is 'a warrior' (v. 3) who acts in power. This unidentified sea, so often a symbol of a chaotic and wild threat to life and/ or to God's creation, here becomes the tool that God uses to bring conquest over the real threat: the 'gods of Egypt', as verse 11 suggests, harking back to the wording of 12:12.

Verses 13–17 unexpectedly cast their gaze forwards, appearing to anticipate some of the wilderness journey to come (including the later Philistines in v. 14), and even ending with reference to the mountain of the Lord and the sanctuary established there (v. 17). This is probably Jerusalem and its temple. The song thus functions as a prophecy as well as a celebration of the past. Note that Miriam is called a prophet as she sings (v. 20) – simple evidence that women could be prophets too.

Verse 19 is a single-verse summary of what they are all singing about. What does it lack? It lacks the passion, the euphoria, the overwhelming relief of deliverance that the song captures so well. Praise often adds so much depth to our story.

6 Manna: daily bread for the journey

Exodus 16:1–21

We are in the section of the book where the people find it easy to complain whenever things are not going smoothly. Already in 14:11–12 they howled with fear and distrust as Pharaoh's army pursued them; in 15:24 they complain that the only drinking water is bitter. The theme of complaint will build in due course to dominate the book of Numbers, later on their wilderness journey.

God's first response, both with the bitter water (15:25) and now with the question of what to eat (v. 4), is to test the Israelites. God will tell them what to do, and if they do it then there will be life – in this case, enough to eat. In many ways, Exodus 16 is like a narrative trial-run for the giving of the law that is coming soon. It is focused on the gift of manna – a word that sounds like the Hebrew for 'what is it?' Presumably that is what they said when they went out in the morning and wondered what this strange gift of food was: fine and flaky, like a kind of bread to eat (vv. 14–15).

The initial rules are simple: take what you need, no more; eat it all, saving none. The passage goes on to increase the complexity: on the sixth day take double, and do not go out to look for it on the seventh day, because that is a sabbath. Interestingly, while those reading from Genesis 2 onwards know that the seventh day is a sabbath – a holy day of 'stopping', of no work – the reference in Exodus 16:23 is the first time anyone in the narrative is told about it. And the sabbath ruling is still to come in chapter 20, of course. So again, this is like a test for what will become shortly the question of obeying the law, which is all about whether Israel can see that the purpose of the law is to bring life.

The core issue here regarding how they approach the daily gift of manna suggests that daily thankfulness, and accepting enough as enough, lies at the heart of seeing God's provision as life-giving and all that we need. The idea is adopted literally, for the same purpose, in Jesus' prayer: give us this day our daily bread.

Guidelines

All through the narrative of the book of Exodus we see God active, overseeing events. That word 'overseeing' has long been used in its Latin form (*pro-video*/providence) to describe God taking charge of human life. And for just as long, people have wondered where that leaves human effort: what kind of agency do humans have in God's world?

If the book of Exodus is to be believed, the answer to this question is: a considerable amount. God intervenes in Israel's suffering by sending Moses (and Aaron) to act on God's behalf – to be (like) a God to Pharaoh, as 7:1 puts it. Hard to imagine a more exalted view of Moses' human effort than that. Then we saw how Pharaoh's innately stubborn 'hard heart' eventually allowed him to have his way – of being stubborn beyond all reasonable judgement. The evidence of history down through the centuries is that powerful leaders unwilling to listen to dissent will indeed go beyond all reasonable judgement. A third example of the same divine/human dynamic was the Israelites being commanded to be still (14:14), and then immediately told to head out towards the as-yet-unparted sea in the next verse. God's work – and human response – go hand-in-hand.

We could multiply examples of this all through the story, and indeed all through the Bible, and that is because this is in general how God works in and through human action. The provision of manna is miraculous, but human effort has to be calibrated to it. The Passover is God's work, but requires faithful human obedience (12:28). And so forth.

God's sovereign initiative and active human participation are not a zero-sum game where the more you have of one, the less you have of the other. Correlating them is the work of prayer – crying out to God so that the divine and the human wills are brought together. The testimony of Exodus is that this happens around God's concern for justice, though not some abstract notion of justice, but a justice that is grounded in God's freely offered love and commitment towards Israel. Even before all this is codified in the ten commandments and the law, it is all there in the narrative of Exodus, celebrating how God's sovereign initiative and full-bodied human response are played out in harmony.

1 Conflict and confrontation

Exodus 17

We are almost at Sinai – Rephidim seems to be the last way-station before it (19:2), and when God stands 'in front of [them]' in verse 6 he is 'at Horeb', which is Sinai. But there is no water. God calls Moses forward to strike a rock to resolve the problem. That image of God 'standing in front of them' probably means that God is available for Moses to talk to, which is just as well since now we have the people testing God, in contrast to the previous chapters where God tested the people.

The way people test the Lord here is captured in the names: in verse 2 Moses asks why the people quarrel and test; and the place where this happened is called in verse 7 Massah ('testing') and Meribah ('quarrelling'). It is recalled in Psalm 95:8, where the psalmist enjoins us not to 'harden our hearts', using one of the words for 'harden' that Exodus uses for this very same phrase that we saw in connection with Pharaoh. Is this a worrying hint that Israel is not as removed from Egypt and its view of the world as it would like to think? (A second water-from-the-rock story in Numbers 20 has a less happy ending for Moses, who perhaps thought that he had learned the trick here in Exodus and could reproduce it on demand, rather than wait for a word from the Lord.)

The second problem in the chapter appears as a military raid on the camp by the Amalekites. The Amalekites are a nation always presented as a threat or enemy to God and God's people. We end with Moses' banner declaring perpetual war with Amalek, and on subsequent appearances (e.g. 1 Samuel 15) the command is still to wipe them out. The story has traditionally been read symbolically: Moses' raised hands indicate prayer; the Amalekites are any 'enemy' (in Jewish tradition: anti-Semites in general); and the battle is the fight against evil – only successful while prayer is (literally) held up. Of course this passage is open to being used to support (religious) violence, but that does not make such an interpretation right.

Oddly, verse 14 is strangely self-defeating: because of this very verse, the memory of Amalek is *not* blotted out. A cautionary word to zealots, perhaps?

2 'You cannot do it alone'

Exodus 18

This rather unexpected interlude seems to be a window into daily life on the wilderness journey, without reference to the ongoing travel, but simply 'encamped at the mountain of God' – Mount Sinai (v. 5), which they do not actually reach until 19:2. We do get some fascinating insights into how Moses operates.

Recall that he married Zipporah, the Midianite, back in chapter 2. Well, according to verse 2 here, he has subsequently sent her away. This phrase later comes to mean 'divorced', though here it is left undefined, but it is clearly not overwhelmingly positive. Her father – Moses' father-in-law – Jethro (who has other names in some passages, e.g. in 2:18 where we first met him), brings her back, along with her two sons. Is it a visit? An intended reunion? Rather strikingly, Moses greets Jethro effusively (v. 7), no mention is made of Zipporah, and then Moses and Jethro 'went into the tent'. We never hear of Zipporah again, and by Numbers 12 Moses has a Cushite (Ethiopian) wife whose black skin colour is part of the focus of that story.

Do we too easily assume that scripture's great 'heroes', even the ones as truly remarkable as Moses, automatically must have had happy family and home situations? Does the family sometimes suffer the cost of a calling as remarkable as Moses' calling? Exodus leaves these questions hanging.

Jethro's main contribution to the ongoing story is to teach Moses the benefits of delegation. Moses is trying every case brought before him and wearing himself out, hence Jethro's words: 'The task is too heavy for you; you cannot do it alone' (v. 18). Variations of this wording are still used today at ordination services or their equivalents.

The way forward is twofold: teach everyone God's standards and appoint capable judges. Note that the requirements for a good judge are to do with their character (v. 21), including fearing God, i.e. living lives dedicated to God. All this good advice comes from a Midianite priest, who also departs the story in the final verse (though see Numbers 10:29–32, where again he bows out).

But Jethro does note that Moses should double-check that this is what God (i.e. Moses' God) wants (v. 23). So: learn wisdom from wherever you can find it, but always bring it before God for testing.

3 'A priestly kingdom and a holy nation'

Exodus 19

First note the nice feature that we are back at Horeb/Sinai, where God had first called Moses in chapter 3. There God had promised that a sign of his promise to Moses was for Moses to worship here after bringing the people out of Egypt (see 3:12). And here he is – so the promise has been kept and we are on track.

Back then, there had been a burning bush and holy ground. Now the whole mountain is holy (v. 12) – again because God is (spectacularly) present (see v. 18) – and this time the whole people have to prepare to be in the presence of holiness.

Moses alone will be called to go up the mountain. What will he hear there? Hard to capture in translation is the vagueness about whether he hears God's voice directly: the Hebrew word *qol* is variously translated in this passage as 'voice', 'thunder', 'blast' and (in chapter 20) 'sound'. Jewish tradition argues over whether Moses heard specific words from God or experienced God in some other (overpowering!) way and then put words to it. The ten commandments may be a word-based exception, but in general it seems likely that it is God's presence that Moses experiences. The speaking God then speaks in and through Moses' words.

A second emphasis in verses 5–6 emphasises that Israel is a 'treasured possession' and 'a priestly kingdom and a holy nation'. Again, translations struggle to pin this down, and many follow the Hebrew more literally: 'kingdom of priests'. But of course it was very clear in Israel who was a priest and who was not, so the meaning of the phrase is probably as the NRSV has it: not that every individual was a priest, but that the nation of Israel was to be 'priestly' with respect to the other nations of the world. Indeed, the next phrase describes it as a 'holy nation' – i.e. a nation set apart.

1 Peter picks up this language to describe God's people: 'a holy priesthood' (1 Peter 2:5). Again the point is not about individual 'priests', but that the whole of God's people is set apart to a priestly role with respect to other people.

Note how in Exodus 19 God is spectacularly separate for the sake of drawing people in. Our calling is similar: separate, for the sake of all.

4 The ten commandments

Exodus 20:1–17

This is one of scripture's most famous passages. Our traditional title comes from 34:28, so we know there must be *ten* commandments (or 'words', as the Hebrew puts it). Numbering the ten has actually proved difficult, and different Christian (and Jewish) traditions do it differently. But on many accounts, note that the first five all name the Lord in their wording (vv. 2–12), while the second five do not (vv. 13–17). This might point to these ten words being tied in to the very specific story of Israel in Exodus, rather than general commandments for all times and places. But on the other hand, the form of these particular ten words does make them stand out from the rest of the laws given in the Old Testament. They are short, relatively context-free and not about detailed aspects of how to legislate or what penalties to impose. In fact they are notably penalty-free.

Clearly, this passage is one key to the Old Testament story. The commandments reveal God's heart for human living. Christians will therefore want to take them extremely seriously – which is not the same as saying that they are a law for Christians.

Note that the tenth commandment prohibits coveting, which is a remarkable pointer to the inner life of a person, even if in practice it may also have meant 'actions that demonstrate covetousness'. It is often observed that you cannot legislate coveting as such. Maybe the 'ten words' were not intended as a law code even in ancient times, but as more of a foundation charter for what good and right living should look like.

Here we meet the sabbath command, properly introduced, after being trialled in chapter 16. It is related to creation, whereas in Deuteronomy 5 it is linked to freedom from slavery. Both are true. Again: deliverance (salvation) and creation are two sides of the same story.

Verse 13 traditionally read 'You shall not kill'. Most (though not all) modern translations say 'murder'. Killing in the Old Testament was clearly sometimes commanded or thought justified – e.g. in legal or military situations. The prohibition is against individually choosing to take life. Here, as with all the commandments, an underlying vision for living rightly – for God – is the key.

5 Freedom to obey the law

Exodus 21:1–27

We select one part of the collections of the laws ('ordinances', v. 1) that take up the remainder of Exodus 20—23, a section of Exodus that has been called 'the covenant code', in part because of 19:5, but also because of how it ends (see 24:7).

One fundamental thing to recognise about this section of scripture is its place in the unfolding narrative of Exodus, where we see Israel being released from slavery in Egypt to pursue the freedom to worship God, and at the moment where they arrive to worship on God's holy mountain (chapter 19; 24:1), the big gift that they receive from God is 'the law'. Most Christians would probably not have anticipated that that would be the gift appropriate to release from slavery, but that may be because Christians have often had an uneasy relationship with Old Testament law.

The word 'law' (*torah*, in Hebrew) means something more like 'instruction'. A faithful Israelite recognised that God's 'law' was a sign of God's love, because it was instruction, or communication, from God, about how best to live. Allied to this, the departure from Egypt left Israel free *from* Egypt, but just as importantly it left them free *for* the calling of serving God. This is not much like the autonomous freedom that some people value today: freedom from all constraints.

Now, of course, this does not mean that any given law in Exodus 20—23 can be plucked out of its context and imagined as a law for today in any straightforward way. But the kinds of moral vision found in these laws still speak to us. Today, verses 2–6 talk about slavery, and it is hard to imagine any form of slavery that could be appropriate today. Yet this passage sees slavery as limited in time (i.e. more like service than ownership), and with the option of a slave loving his master so that he might wish to stay in his service. In some ways, this 'slavery' was more like an assumed social structure where some people worked for others.

Finally, we may note that the 'eye for an eye' ruling (v. 24 and elsewhere) is about limiting revenge. Also, remarkably, it applies to all classes. Biblical law sows some revolutionary seeds.

6 Signed, sealed and delivered

Exodus 24

God invites Moses, Aaron and certain others up the mountain to 'worship at a distance': it is an invitation to a covenant meal. A covenant is a formal commitment between two people or groups, in this case God and Israel. The most famous example of a covenant today is a marriage – where two people enter into binding commitments that change their status with regard to each other. Here, Israel commits to being God's people, in the sense now outlined in the 'law' (revelation) that has just been set out in chapters 20—23. God's commitment to Israel is also now clear (see also 23:20–33), not that it will not be tested in the stories to come.

Covenants were agreed in the ancient world over a meal – rather like the meal that celebrates a wedding today perhaps. In verses 9–11 we read that Moses, Aaron and co sit with God and eat and drink. The narrator may be a little nervous here. It was widely understood that you could not see God and live (as is said in 33:20). But here, the participants in the meal seem to be within striking distance of seeing God (v. 10), even if the story emphasises the pavement under God's feet. The gist of these wonderful verses is: they ate with God, and lived to tell the tale!

One key development remains for the book of Exodus to conclude: the building of a holy place where God might dwell in the midst of the people, and thereby avoiding the problem of God's holiness being too overpowering for them. It is to learn how to do this that Moses disappears into the cloud of God's glory at the top of Mount Sinai at the end of the chapter. Those who read on will experience seven chapters describing how to build the tabernacle. They may not always make exciting reading, but their length and detail are intended to emphasise how important it is.

It turns out that the rest of the people will take this occasion to put that gold plundered from the Egyptians to an unexpected use, in building a golden calf. So the story will continue – still in pursuit of true worship of the true God, still journeying on, even today.

Guidelines

We started by saying Exodus was the greatest sequel ever told. Remarkably it holds together two things that are often allowed to drift apart: the release from the danger and difficulty that oppresses them at the beginning of the book, and then the long hard look beyond 'the happy ending' of liberation, to the kind of life that Israel might now live. This is like a Hollywood film starting out with rescue and escape, bringing the key players together in joyous union around the middle of the plot, and then ending with lengthy meetings about what they are going to do next, interspersed with stories of spectacular failure (the golden calf). Or in other words: it is like no Hollywood film ever (with the debatable exception of the *Star Wars* sequel, *The Empire Strikes Back*).

In fact, Exodus is only a book in a limited sense. It is actually part of a longer, ongoing narrative that will extend through further focus on holiness (in Leviticus) and picking up the wilderness wandering narrative (in Numbers), where complaint and startling divine intervention resume in full. But the course is set. The world that Israel leaves behind – slavery in Egypt – is not the real focus. We actually learned rather little about it, speaking historically. No Pharaohs were named, no pyramids were mentioned, no great Egyptian literature was quoted. It was simply the place of slavery where God delivered Israel from injustice and suffering. It serves as a negative picture of being enslaved.

But the real focus is the strange, challenging, positive picture of being enslaved to God. Israel's freedom is freedom to serve the Lord. This story, like all Old Testament stories, was written for us (Romans 15:4) – not just to inform us historically, which is why we do not mind missing out on all that historical information, but to portray for us the core issues of what life with God is all about. For Christians, the freedom of being in Christ is the freedom to serve Christ. We might *think* we would rather do our own thing, on the grounds that we know better. The book of Exodus resolutely insists: we do not. We need God's instruction (*torah*; 'law') to live rightly. That way lies true freedom – then, and now.

FURTHER READING

David Fleer and Dave Bland (eds.), *Reclaiming the Imagination: The exodus as paradigmatic narrative for preaching* (Chalice Press, 2009).

Terence E. Fretheim, *Exodus* (John Knox Press, 1991).

Victor P. Hamilton, *Exodus: An exegetical commentary* (Baker Academic, 2011).

Mark Scarlata, *The Abiding Presence: A theological commentary on Exodus* (SCM Press, 2018).

John's gospel: face to face with Jesus

Terry Griffith

Our focus will be on the characters and figures that surround Jesus in John's gospel. There are about 70 individuals and groups portrayed by John. Some merely act as functionaries necessary for the telling of the story, but many participate in the progressive unfolding of the plot. This is primarily, but not exclusively, conveyed through the dialogues that characterise this gospel. These encounters provide a wider-angle lens on the character of Jesus himself, as well as revealing a varied range of possible responses to him. Such character portrayals engage our imagination afresh as we identify (or not) with them.

The prologue (1:1–18) describes Jesus as the 'Word' but avoids presenting this as a static principle. The Word was 'with' (*pros*) God and some paraphrase this as 'face to face with' God, an intimacy brought out in verse 18 (literally 'in the bosom of the Father') and which enables the revelation of the Father (14:9). The participants in the story do not know Jesus from this perspective and often misunderstand his identity, teaching and mission. However, it is through their being face to face with Jesus that the prologue's truths are fleshed out. Each character thus contributes towards achieving John's aim that 'you may believe that Jesus is the Christ [Messiah], the Son of God, and that by believing you may have life in his name' (20:31).

In these readings each player adds to the thrust and impact of the whole gospel drama. George Herbert (1593–1633) expresses it well in his poem *The Holy Scriptures II*:

Oh that I knew how all thy lights combine,
*   And the configurations of their glorie!*
*   Seeing not onely how each verse doth shine,*
But all the constellations of the storie.

Unless otherwise stated, Bible quotations are taken from the ESV.

1 John (the Baptist)

John 1:1–39

John's gospel begins with 'the Word', but this chapter is dominated by another John who simply calls himself 'the voice' (v. 23). In fact, no earthly character in this gospel is ascribed more direct speech than John. He is the first named character and the first to speak, and like Jesus he is said to be 'sent from God' (v. 6). Interestingly, the ancient manuscripts have no paragraph marker at verse 19 and give no indication that the 'prologue' (vv. 1–18) is set off from the body of this gospel. The story of this John is thus intricately bound up with the story of 'the Word'. Yet, although he is 'the voice', no verbal interaction is recorded between John and Jesus.

John's John is not portrayed as the proclaimer of repentance and so is never called 'the Baptist'. His primary role is as a truthful witness to the identity and mission of Jesus (5:33). This idea is emphasised seven times in our passage (vv. 7, 8, 15, 19, 32, 34). The multifaceted nature of John's witness is conveyed through his baptising (v. 25; 3:23); heralding (vv. 23, 29); teaching (3:26, 'Rabbi'; 10:41); his role as best man (3:29); and his illumination (5:35).

The contours of John's ministry are set out early on and are later elaborated. He was not the light (vv. 8a, 19–21; 3:28); he came to bear witness to the light (vv. 8b, 29–36; 3:26; 5:33); he bore witness to the light so that all might believe (vv. 7b, 35–37; 10:41–42); and he is subordinate to Jesus (vv. 15, 27, 30; 3:28–30). John's testimony introduced in the prologue is thus amplified in the rest of John 1, recapitulated in John 3, approved in John 5 and shown as effective in John 10. John is thus portrayed as loyal and faithful to Jesus and bold in his affirmation of Jesus as Israel's Messiah (v. 23), the Lamb of God (v. 29), the baptiser with the Holy Spirit (v. 33) and the Son of God/chosen one (v. 34). Both John's humility before Christ and obedience to God (vv. 29–34) are also highlighted. John serves to carry forward the message of the prologue and, while never said to 'believe', these traits combine to make him a model disciple whose witness is true (5:33). Indeed, John's uncompromising voice put him in prison (3:24). Would there be enough evidence to put us there with him?

2 The mother of Jesus

John 1:40—2:12; 19:25–27

Various disciples have acknowledged Jesus as Israel's Messiah (1:41, 45, 49) and this group now accompany Jesus and his mother to the wedding in Cana (2:1–2). It is a curiosity of John's gospel that the name of Jesus' mother is simply assumed. The epithet is sufficient to identify her. Her words are few, but her importance in the story is signalled by the fact that she is the first to be introduced and to speak.

It is not stated why Mary takes up the responsibility of sparing the bride-groom's shame in not providing enough wine for the wedding party. But like many mothers, she has a plan. Her statement to Jesus is an implied request and Jesus' reply, though enigmatic, emboldens Mary to instruct the servants (2:3–5). Jesus' address to his mother, 'Woman' (2:4; 19:26; see also 4:21; 20:15), and his response (literally 'what to me and to you?') create a sense of dissonance and distance. Jesus feels that it is not the time to go public. And yet Jesus does comply and in fact enhances the bridegroom's honour (2:6–10). However, he does so in a way that his own honour (glory) is revealed only to those who know the inside story, namely, his disciples, who are said to believe in him (2:11). Surely Mary is included here, and her association with the disciples is accordingly highlighted (2:12).

By contrast, at the cross Mary says nothing (19:25–27). She is a passive witness. At the foot of the cross, her relationship with her son is now put on a different footing as Jesus fulfils his Father's mission. From this point on, Mary is to have no claim upon Jesus as her son, as Jesus entrusts her to another within the household of faith. Mary is thus always associated with Jesus' disciples, whether at Cana, Capernaum or Jerusalem. This is her new family now.

At Cana, Mary acts as a catalyst to Jesus' ministry with her plan. She is an active agent, seeing, intervening and instructing. It is almost as if Jesus is cooperating with her. At Calvary, however, only Jesus speaks and his words are to be received in faith and obedience. It is Jesus who has the greater plan that his mother and the disciple whom he loved must act upon. Now, as then, the cross of Christ must be the basis for gathering the family of God.

3 Nicodemus

John 2:13—3:21; 7:50–52; 19:38–42

Passover brings Jesus to Jerusalem, where his actions draw him to the attention of the religious authorities (2:13–22). However, one influential Pharisee, Nicodemus, concludes that Jesus is a teacher 'from God' because of the signs he does (2:23—3:2). He approaches Jesus privately and by night, which provides a foil for John's motif of light and darkness (3:19–21). Jesus immediately asserts his authority by resetting the discussion topic to seeing and entering the kingdom of God (3:3). Although Nicodemus was *the* 'teacher of Israel' (3:10), he gets everything wrong. He mistakes Jesus' notion of a spatial ('from above') and spiritual ('of the Spirit') begetting, for a temporal ('a second time') and fleshly ('womb') birth (3:4–8). Nicodemus thus exemplifies those who are 'from the earth' (3:31) and are 'of this world' (8:23) and who do not receive Jesus' testimony and believe (3:10–15). He just disappears into the darkness of night, but this is not the last we hear of him.

When the officers sent by the Sanhedrin to arrest Jesus return empty-handed, Nicodemus intervenes on a point of justice. The officers, having heard Jesus (7:46), felt unable to apprehend him, whereas the 'court' which is yet to hear him has already concluded the matter. Nicodemus' implied defence of Jesus earns him the riposte, 'Are you from Galilee too?' (7:52). Although it remains the case that no authoritative figure is known to believe in Jesus (7:48), at least Nicodemus 'does what is true' (3:21a). An element of ambiguity has been introduced.

Nicodemus finally appears with Joseph of Arimathea, who is described as a secret disciple of Jesus (19:38). However, what they do together is done very publicly and in daylight (3:21). John has repeatedly emphasised the kingship of Jesus in his passion narrative, and the sheer amount of precious spices that Nicodemus brings befits a royal burial (19:39). Now that Jesus has been lifted up, perhaps he has indeed drawn Nicodemus to himself (3:14–15; 12:32–33). You know someone by the company they keep and whom they seek to honour (5:44). Is Nicodemus a case where truthful actions speak louder than words? The decision to become a disciple of Jesus is rarely straightforward or clear-cut. Do we need to cut seekers after truth some slack while they find their way to the cross of Christ?

4 The Samaritan woman

John 4:4–42

Jesus returns to Cana in Galilee (4:46) via Samaria, where he meets an unnamed woman by Jacob's well near Sychar. The contrast between Nicodemus' response to Jesus and this woman's could hardly be greater, and perhaps this is the point. The danger, however, is that of introducing our own prejudices by reading between the lines of this encounter. So much depends on nuances of intonation and gesture, to which we have no access. The storyteller's art is actually seen in a word which is often left untranslated where verse 6 literally reads, 'he sat down *like this* by the well'. We could do with some more help here. Was she an immoral woman or a victim of circumstance? Was she ashamed or feisty? Was she evasive or curious? Was she confused or astute? What assumptions have you brought to this woman?

Here we have a rarity, a theological debate between a woman and a man over two differing religious traditions. From the Samaritan woman's point of view (v. 9) Jesus is a Judean (the meaning 'Jew' comes from this). Now if we take as her starting point that this was *Jacob's* well (v. 12), the discussion revolves not so much around (mis)understanding the nature of water (vv. 13–15) but claims about the validity of competing Samaritan and Jewish religious traditions. The topic then moves naturally to the place where God may be truly worshipped (v. 20). However, Jesus moves the question from the topographical to a universal plane when he defines worship in terms of spirit and truth (vv. 21–24).

This development evokes in the woman the hope of the Messiah to which both traditions looked. For the first time Jesus makes a direct claim which in Greek literally reads, 'I am, who speaks to you' (v. 26). At this, she returns to her village and provokes their interest by claiming she might have found the Messiah (v. 29: 'Come, see', as in 1:39, 46). She thus proves herself to be both perceptive and responsive, and an initiator and persuader. She does what the disciples never thought to do (v. 8), for the whole village now approaches Jesus and comes to the conviction that this man is 'the Saviour of the World' (v. 42). He is no mere prophet (v. 19) but the anticipated Messiah, and the gospel's stated purpose (20:31) is indeed fulfilled here of all places!

5 The Jews

John 5:1–24, 31–47

The believing responses of the Samaritans (4:39–42) and the royal official's household (4:53) are followed by the somewhat lame response of the healed invalid (vv. 1–15). In fact, belief is replaced by unbelief, rejection and hostility as the first direct confrontation between Jesus and 'the Jews' is provoked by this sabbath healing (vv. 8–10). The hostility of 'the Jews', who act as a corporate personality in the story, is the dynamic that will dominate the rest of John's gospel. They are so incensed by Jesus' words and actions that they seek to have him killed (vv. 16–18). Furthermore, Jesus' appeal to the authority for his work as the Son was hardly calculated to endear himself to them (vv. 19–24). Indeed, in a tour de force, Jesus accuses them of being deaf to God's voice, blind to God's form, bankrupt in God's word, ignorant of God's Son, strangers to God's love, disdainful of God's honour and disobedient to God's prophet (vv. 37–47).

It is vital, therefore, to delineate carefully the identity of this group, given the history of anti-Semitic interpretation and application of John's description of 'the Jews'. Previously, they have been described as 'from Jerusalem' with authority to send priests and Levites (1:19), who later are said to have 'been sent from the Pharisees' (1:24, the better translation). We next find 'the Jews' in the temple challenging Jesus' actions there (2:18, 20), and Nicodemus is described as a Pharisee and 'a ruler of the Jews' (3:1).

The Jerusalem location of this chapter (v. 1) is important, for it is not the fact of being Jewish that is being highlighted. Jesus himself is a 'Jew' (4:9) and he affirms that 'salvation is from the Jews' (4:22). Many contexts thus point to 'the Jews' as a term referring to temple loyalists comprising the religious authorities. And yet there are hints that even some from this group come to believe Jesus (12:42; 19:38–42), while the term is also used more generally of others who also believe (11:45; 12:11). We must not rush to judgement on John. Religious power structures lie behind John's pejorative uses of 'the Jews'. The religious-theological conflict with the Pharisees will, in due course, develop into a religious-political conflict with the chief priests. Merely partisan and institutional religion should carry a spiritual health warning.

6 The Twelve

For the first time 'the Twelve' are distinguished as the core of a wider group also known as '[Jesus'] disciples' (6:66–67). They had assisted in the feeding miracle that begins John 6 and set off at the end of the day by boat without Jesus for Capernaum. En route they encountered a storm, but it was what happened next that terrified them. The other gospels supply the detail that they thought they were seeing a ghost on the water, perhaps of a drowned man. However, their fears were allayed by the welcome realisation that it was only (!) Jesus approaching the boat (vv. 16–21).

Little is made of their reaction to Jesus until after the synagogue sermon in Capernaum the following day (v. 59). The crowd's expectation after the feeding miracle that Jesus is a Moses figure (see 6:14–15) is shredded by his exposition of the manna from heaven. Jesus is not only the bread of God/life come down from heaven, but in order to gain the life he offers they must also eat his flesh and drink his blood (vv. 53–56). It is difficult to underestimate the shockwave that would have passed through the congregation at this point.

What happens next is significant, as John focuses on the post-sermon analysis among 'his disciples' (v. 60). Not only do many grumble about this hard doctrine, but they are also offended. Their disgust is followed by desertion as the wider group of the disciples divides over Jesus' doctrine. It is at this point that the Twelve are distinguished and distinguish themselves. Peter's first words in this gospel are a remarkable declaration of their loyalty to Jesus and faith in his teaching (v. 68). They have participated in the feeding miracle, picked Jesus up on the lake, are persuaded by his teaching and perceive him to be the Holy One of God. And yet Jesus says that one of the dozen is dirty! The Twelve will all prove to be an ambiguous lot as the story unfolds. They believe and are afraid, know and misunderstand, abide with and desert Jesus. Being a disciple is about a willingness to be taught by God (6:45), not having all the answers. The character and teaching of Jesus still continue to offend us two millennia later. To what extent do our responses reflect those of the Twelve and this wider group of Jesus' disciples?

Guidelines

Almost a century ago, Rabbi Dr Israel Abrahams wrote: 'To us Jews the Fourth Gospel is the most Jewish of the four.' This observation may come as a surprise, but the discovery of the Dead Sea Scrolls further confirmed the Jewish character of this gospel, whose narrative framework is structured around Judaism's festivals in Jerusalem. It also draws upon Old Testament motifs such as the temple, the brazen serpent and manna, and presents their fulfilment through Jesus. While John's gospel has a very different feel to that of the others (with their much greater focus on Galilee), it is certainly not less Jewish, let alone anti-Jewish as some have asserted, for all that.

Of the ideas introduced in the opening verses of John's gospel, perhaps none is thematically more important than that of witness. John's Jesus is portrayed as conducting a lawsuit with the world, in which he calls forward witnesses to his true identity. Of the 47 occurrences in this gospel of the Greek verb and noun for witness/testimony (the root of our English word 'martyr'), 28 occur in the first five chapters. These witnesses include John (the Baptist), the words of Jesus (3:32), the Samaritan woman (4:39), the works of Jesus (5:36), the Father (5:37) and the scriptures (5:39). The Holy Spirit (1:32) and the disciples (1:14) will also be called as witnesses in due course (15:26–27).

John's dualistic worldview finds expression, for example, in the conflict between light and darkness (1:5; 3:19–21), or the antithesis of 'from above'/'of the earth' (3:31). However, we must not allow this to push us into a black-and-white approach to characterisation. The characters are not mere cardboard cut-outs without depth, or static types that define individuals as 'goodies' or 'baddies' with no admixture of these qualities or possibility of change. John is much more nuanced than that, and characters have the opportunity to develop as they remain accountable in their face-to-face encounters with Jesus. Indeed, the characters he portrays and the stories he narrates illustrate how the decisions that his readers are called to make about Jesus do have eternal consequences in terms of life or death (3:36; 5:24–29). How far do you think John has succeeded in his aims?

8–14 August

1 The crowd

John 7:1–44

Without the aid of social media, Jesus had gathered a huge following within Palestine. He has already addressed crowds in Galilee, but the festival crowd in

Jerusalem (pilgrims drawn from many places) takes on a group-oriented personality and shared identity as pious Jews. The Judaean setting is significant for, although Jesus has disciples there (v. 3), it forms the context where for the first time 'the world' is used in a hostile sense (v. 7; see 1:10–11). However, 'the crowd' is carefully distinguished from 'the Jews' whom the crowd is said to fear (vv. 11–13) and some Jerusalemites also distinguish themselves from the religious authorities (vv. 25–26), a distinction reciprocated with disdain (7:49).

The crowd, true to type, proves to be a mixed bunch, and their varied responses advance the plot by sharpening the issue of Jesus' identity. Some think he is a good man, while others describe him in theologically loaded terms as a deceiver (v. 12) and even possessed by a demon (v. 20). The question of messiahship is very much abroad, but it further divides opinion as some are said to believe in Jesus (v. 31) while others are doubtful (vv. 25–26). Jesus' very public invitation at the feast to come to him (and by implication not to the temple) as the fountain of life (vv. 37–38), results in further consternation. Different groups conclude that he must be the prophet or Messiah, or that he cannot be such, or that the time has come to arrest Jesus and shut him up (vv. 40–44).

It remains unclear whether anyone in the crowd has truly believed in Jesus. We can detect a certain sympathy, an enthusiasm probably borne along by patriotism and at least some theological discernment. There is potential for belief and discipleship, but present also are misunderstanding, rejection and unbelief. The crowd is a complex entity but in the end seems consistent in its inability to make up its mind. It has frequently been thus over the identity of Jesus. Many have admired him or even been convinced to some extent of his claims but will not stand out and be counted. Others have hated his guts. The majority remain indifferent. It's easy for us to take the moral high ground and assume that we would not have belonged to this crowd. Pray appropriately for someone you know who does.

2 The apostates

John 8:30–59

John 8 continues to highlight differing assessments of Jesus' claims, and a significant number believe in Jesus (v. 30). However, what is most striking about this chapter is what happens next. It seems psychologically unconvincing that verse 31 refers to the group who have just been described as believing in Jesus, because seven verses later Jesus accuses them of wanting to kill him, thereby provoking the most vitriolic exchange in John's gospel. As Greek has no pluperfect active participle, the perfect participle takes on double duty and verse 31 can be understood accordingly, 'To the Jews who had believed in him (but did so no longer)'; just as in John 11:44, '[Lazarus] who had died (but was dead no longer)'. John often couples responses of belief and unbelief, so which group is being referred to in verse 31? The most obvious candidates are those Galilean 'disciples' (a word last used in 7:3 of Jerusalemite 'disciples') who 'turned back and no longer walked with him' (6:66). Former disciples of Jesus, as loyal Jews, would naturally also be present at the feast.

Their presence explains the apparent shift in outlook and they do indeed attempt to kill Jesus (v. 59). Jesus reserves his strongest language for them. They belong to their 'father the devil', who is a 'murderer' and a 'liar' from the beginning (vv. 41–44). Interestingly, in John's first letter, those who have denied that Jesus is the Messiah and have abandoned the Christian community are described as 'antichrists', 'liars', 'of the devil' and 'murderers' (1 John 2:18–22; 3:8, 15). Questions of identity raise very strong feelings.

This group looks to Abraham, the father of the Jewish nation, as a badge of their identity (vv. 39, 53). They had looked to Jesus for something which had not been delivered to their satisfaction and they, in turn, accuse him of being a bastard Samaritan and demon possessed (vv. 41, 48). Jesus' concluding reply raises the identity stakes to the highest level possible with the startling, 'before Abraham was, I am' (v. 58). Jesus' strongest language is not aimed at the Jews as such, whom Jesus identifies rather with 'the world' (15:18—16:4), but at those who had followed him and have abandoned their allegiance to him. Betrayal was the hardest thing Jesus had to deal with. Do you agree?

3 The man born blind

John 9

Jesus seamlessly passes through the chapter division (some manuscripts adding a 'like this') into the space where those excluded from the temple might beg. His statement about being the light of the world (8:12a) has not yet been expounded. However, the healing of a congenitally blind man provides the opportunity needed to illustrate the themes of light and darkness (8:12b; vv. 4–5) and the place of sin (vv. 2, 41). There are some peculiarities in this busy chapter. Jesus is the only named character; the only direct mention of the disciples in chapters 7—10 is in verse 2 of this chapter; Jesus' absence between verses 8 and 35 is the longest in John's gospel; and the '(in)sightful' man has more dialogue than nearly all other characters in this gospel. What is going on here?

The whole narrative serves to draw the man into a close identification with Jesus in several ways. They are both regarded as sinners (vv. 24, 34); both use sarcasm to similar effect (3:10; v. 30); and both hold their theological ground with an authoritative use of 'we know' (3:11; v. 31). The man's journey to faith in Jesus (in contrast to the blind man in 5:1–15) is well mapped. It begins with (blind) obedience to 'the man called Jesus' (v. 11) and then recognises him as 'a prophet' (v. 17) who must be 'from God' (v. 33). It finishes when Jesus searches him out and he actually sees Jesus for the first time. He confesses Jesus as 'the Son of Man' and 'Lord' and worships him (vv. 35–38). The man has shown himself to be obedient, feisty, able to testify to experience, theologically adept and willing to face ostracism for Jesus' sake.

The Pharisees, however, never get beyond seeing the man as blindly ignorant and so they come under judgement from Jesus. Their line of questioning leads them in an ever-spiralling descent into the darkness of sin and guilt, while they remain ignorant of the one God has sent (vv. 4, 39–41). Ironically, their questioning has actually pushed the man towards Jesus! Their journey from sight to blindness is thus as profound as the man's journey from blindness to sight. This unnamed man shows us that it is not having all the answers that matters to God, but testifying to what we know of Jesus.

4 The shepherd

John 10:1–39

The ramifications arising from the healing of the blind man are not yet over (v. 21). The Pharisees, as blind watchmen or shepherds (Isaiah 56:10–11), have ejected one of the sheep of Israel (9:34), but the good shepherd has sought and found this sheep (9:35). The blind man, at first, would only have been able to recognise Jesus by his voice (9:7; vv. 3–4). However, the Pharisees who have been able to see Jesus all along refuse to listen to that voice (vv. 26–27).

The character of Jesus is indirectly indicated through an extended pastoral figure of speech (v. 6). It is not difficult to imagine who the thieves, robbers, hired hands and wolves might be. His imagery, laden with the language of boundaries and thresholds, represents a challenge to the gatekeepers of the synagogue (9:22). Jesus proclaims himself to be the gate, as well as the good shepherd who leads his sheep in and out of the fold (v. 9). He is even willing to cross the threshold of death and return for them (vv. 17–18).

Like Marmite, Jesus again divides opinion (v. 19). The storm that has been brewing comes to a head at the Feast of Dedication (note that in verse 36 Jesus is described as dedicated to the Father in his mission to the world). This confrontation in Solomon's Colonnade takes on the atmosphere of a courtroom drama as 'the Jews' find Jesus guilty of blasphemy. But Jesus is the judge here (acting like the shepherd kings of Israel), who has already pronounced a guilty verdict upon the Pharisees (9:39–41). The demand for proof constitutes the charge (v. 24). Jesus' defence is that the evidence is there to see for those who have eyes to see (v. 25). The reason for their blindness is their unbelief, which constitutes a counter-charge (v. 26). As they do not hear the shepherd's voice, they must fall into the category of thieves and wolves who attempt to snatch his sheep from his grasp. Indeed, he will protect his sheep and provide them with eternal life (vv. 27–29, 10). It is Jesus' claims to deity that finally provoke 'the Jews' to seize the shepherd, but he eludes them (vv. 30–39). Jesus will not be found again within the temple in John's gospel. We, too, have the shepherd's words, but do we hear his voice?

5 Martha

John 11:1–44

Martha belongs to a family that holds a special place in Jesus' heart (v. 5). While John 11 is known for Lazarus, he speaks not a word and performs just one shuffling action (v. 44). However, his resurrection, or more strictly his resuscitation (for he will die again), becomes political dynamite (12:9–11). It is easy to overlook the description of him as 'he *whom you love* is ill' (v. 3, emphasis mine). Lazarus is not defined by his illness (nor by any other circumstance) but by the fact that he is beloved (v. 5). It is worth pausing and considering that this is true of us all in Christ.

No adjectives describe Martha or adverbs her actions. The focus is on her speech. She calls Jesus 'Teacher' and 'Lord' (vv. 21, 28) and this confirms she is his disciple. She goes out to greet Jesus on his arrival and some interpret her first words as an implied rebuke, 'If you had been here, my brother would not have died' (v. 21), but could it not rather be read as a statement of faith? The messenger bringing the news about Lazarus would surely have returned immediately with Jesus' response, 'This illness does not lead to death' (v. 4). Of course, by the time this gets back to Bethany, Lazarus would already have died (v. 39). Martha's 'But even now I know' (v. 22), though remarkable, is not therefore entirely unexpected. It communicates certainty and confidence in Jesus rather than grief and disappointment.

Martha believes in the future resurrection, but Jesus draws her attention to himself, who guarantees this by virtue of his being the resurrection and life (vv. 23–25). This personal revelation requires her personal response (v. 26). Martha delivers in spades as she makes the purest Johannine confession of faith possible (v. 27; 20:31). However, having presumably laid out Lazarus' body and now faced with the stark reality of his death, she seems to stumble at the tomb (v. 39). Jesus' reference to seeing the glory of God (v. 40) takes us back to what was previously communicated back to her (v. 4). That promise, and its fulfilment in answer to the thunderous command, 'Lazarus, come out!' (v. 43), lays Martha's fears (and ours) to rest. In fact, the earliest pictograms in the Christian catacombs in Rome are of Jesus and Lazarus. All Christian funerals are services of hope, and in this regard the contrast with humanist funerals could not be more stark.

6 Mary

John 11:45—12:11, 20–33

Mary speaks only once, echoing Martha's words (11:32), but she is found at Jesus' feet twice (11:32; 12:3). And yet Mary speaks volumes through these acts of devotion. Her weeping prepares the way for Jesus' weeping (11:33–35) and her anointing anticipates his burial (12:7). It might be that Mary intended this as an extravagant expression of thanksgiving for the restoration of her brother. Howsoever offered, Jesus not only permits Mary this costly and intimate act of devotion, but also commends and interprets it as an expression of deep love and theological insight. Hers is a dramatised confession of faith as she makes the most of her opportunity before his entry into Jerusalem. All theology should be an expression of devotion and worship and leave a lingering scent of fragrant perfume (12:3). I am reminded of my theology tutor, Bruce Milne, who began each of his lectures with prayer that often led me into the felt sense of Jesus' presence.

While Martha's exchange with Jesus focused on resurrection and life, Mary's response focuses on grieving and death. Indeed, Mary's act forms part of a sequence anticipating the passion of Jesus, coming, as it does, between the words of Caiaphas and of Jesus. If Mary may be said to prepare Jesus for his death by a prophetic action, then Caiaphas proposes Jesus' death with a prophetic word as he engineers what is likely to have been a formal resolution of the Sanhedrin (11:53). Ironically, Caiaphas says more than he realises in his substitutionary rationalisation for this decision (11:49–52).

It is left to Jesus to proclaim the rich and deep significance of his imminent death (12:23). It will have cosmic and universal consequences in terms of judgement and salvation. His being lifted up from the earth will mark both the demise of the prince of this world and the drawing of humankind to himself (12:31–33). Moreover, it is through these achievements that both the Father and Son will be glorified, and this is confirmed by the only direct words spoken by God in John's gospel (12:27–28). There are also practical consequences for our discipleship. If we are to glorify God, then it is only by imitating and following Jesus that we shall do this and so find ourselves in the place where his Father will honour us (12:24–26).

Guidelines

The end of what is known as the 'Book of Signs' has been reached. What now lies ahead is often described as the 'Book of Glory'. This is a somewhat artificial distinction given that the summary purpose of the signs is not stated towards the end (20:31), and that the theme of glory is found in the prologue (1:14). However, John 12:37–50 does constitute a fitting summary of Jesus' public ministry and draws together important Johannine themes.

First, the theme of faith is taken up with John's characteristic portrayal of the duality of decision (12:37–39, 42–46). Second, the theme of revelation is emphasised by the contrast between sight/light and blindness/darkness (12:38, 40–41, 45–46). John omits the reference to deafness in the Isaiah quotation to further underscore this. Ironically, it is the Greeks who would 'see Jesus' (12:21) but not 'his own' (1:11). Third, the theme of glory is highlighted in a remarkable way when none other than Isaiah is credited with seeing Jesus' glory (doxa), which is about as high a Christology as any to be found in this gospel, given the setting of Isaiah's vision within the temple (12:41; Isaiah 6:1). Fourth, the guilt of many of the religious leaders is established because they had no regard to the praise (doxa) which comes from God (12:43). Finally, the themes of eternal life and condemnation are explored in terms of the acceptance or rejection of Jesus himself and his words (12:47–50). This is the measure by which the varied responses of the Johannine characters are to be evaluated.

Rudolf Bultmann, the famous German New Testament scholar of a previous generation, got almost everything wrong about John's gospel, but the one thing he saw more clearly than most was that this gospel is a call to decision par excellence. Have we made, and do we continue to make, the decision to believe or not, to see or remain in darkness, to look for God's praise rather than human praise, and to anticipate the verdict of the last day in the way we accept or reject Jesus and his word right now? To be persuaded of these things is what it takes to be a true witness according to John. If the church does not bear witness to *this* Jesus, who will?

1 Simon Peter and Judas

John 13:1–38

Simon Peter is the most frequently mentioned and the most complex of the disciples. At his first meeting he was given another name by Jesus meaning 'rock', indicating strength and stability (1:42). With his first words, a confident confession of faith, we find him acting as a spokesman for the twelve (6:68–69). However, the fault lines and weaknesses in his character begin to emerge. The introduction of the beloved disciple into the narrative from this point onwards further serves to highlight Peter's failings (vv. 23–25).

Each detail of Jesus' actions is etched in the disciples' memory (vv. 3–5, 12). The laying aside and putting on of his outer garments recall the exact same verbs used of the good shepherd who lays down his life and takes it up again (10:17). Jesus hereby demonstrates the salvific and ethical shape of his calling as the suffering servant and shepherd Messiah. Meanwhile, the significance of what Jesus is doing in washing his disciples' feet is lost on them all. Foot-washing quintessentially defines the master/servant relationship, but Jesus inverts it (vv. 12–17). This is what wrong-foots Peter. Perhaps the others were stunned into silence, but Peter impetuously both questions and reprimands Jesus, and in so doing ironically takes up the master's role in seeking to instruct Jesus (vv. 8–9). We cannot doubt Peter's sincerity as he (perhaps typically) overreacts, but we begin to question his spiritual insight (vv. 9–10).

The fullness of Jesus' knowledge (vv. 1–3, 11) sets in stark contrast the disciples' ignorance (vv. 7, 12, 22–23). Peter in particular fails to grasp Jesus' elusive actions and enigmatic words as he tries to assume the role of the good shepherd who will lay down his life for Jesus (v. 37). Jesus' reply demolishes Peter's courageous but mistaken protestation and casts doubt on his loyalty. Peter will indeed follow Jesus, but this will only lead him to the point of experiencing pained anguish and bitter shame as he fulfils Jesus' prophecy (v. 38). However, the story will reveal that he is no diabolically inspired Judas who enters the darkness never to emerge from it (vv. 2, 11, 27–30; 18:2–3). John's narrative skill shows that Jesus remains in full control throughout, and by his grace Simon, despite his failure, will indeed become 'Peter'. Reflect on how much you see of yourself in Peter's story.

2 Jesus and the Holy Spirit

John 14:1–4, 15–31; 15:18–27

The focus moves from the washing of dirty feet to the calming of troubled hearts (14:1, 27). The narrative space also becomes much more intimate, with the start of the 'farewell discourse'. These few hours with his disciples, where narrative time seems to stand still, are important because Jesus brings them face to face with the future. The cause of anxiety is Jesus' talk of 'going (away)' and 'leaving' (14:2–4, 12, 18–19, 28). This is countered by his talk of 'coming (again)' and 'seeing (him)' (14:3, 18–19). There is a lot of focus upon Jesus' travel plans, but the itinerary and destination are not clear to the disciples.

The key to a future without Jesus' own presence is the promise of 'another Helper' (14:16). The Greek word is *paraclete*, which is also used of Jesus in 1 John 2:2. Both a continuity and discontinuity is communicated by the word 'another'. The precise meaning of *paraclete* as applied to the Holy Spirit is more difficult to pin down. The translation 'advocate' has been used, which seems to fit with the courtroom drama setting where witnesses are called for the defence. The Spirit of truth does indeed both witness and help the disciples to witness to Jesus (15:26–27). However, *paraclete* was never used in legal settings in this way. What the defendant needed was someone of standing to identify with them so that their presence beside them, without a word being uttered, spoke volumes in their defence (14:16–17, 23). In Roman courts it was not so much your lawyer but who stood by you that counted.

A Russian Baptist pastor, a friend of mine, tells how his father was exiled from Moscow to Tula for his religious activities. Undaunted, while founding a new church, he was regularly called in by the KGB and harassed. His ten-year-old son wrote a letter to the General Secretary of the Communist Party, Nikita Khrushchev, asking why his father, a good man, was being treated this way. When his father was next called in by the KGB, he was told he would be left alone because he had 'a friend in high places'. This is the role of the Helper or Counsellor, who brings assurance, confidence and protection in the face of whatever opposition we may face (15:18–27).

3 The world and the Father

John 16:19—17:26

The sense of denouement is conveyed by the increased use of 'now' in these chapters. The concept of 'the world' (*kosmos*) also comes to the fore, with half of the gospel's occurrences found in John 13—17 and almost one quarter in John 17 alone. The term 'world' as used by John refers positively to the created order, the material realm into which Jesus entered or the object of God's love and salvific purpose. However, it also appears as a pejorative term for humanity organised in hostile opposition to God. As such, the 'world' is not merely the backdrop for Jesus' story but also becomes a character on the stage.

The world is characterised by the darkness of ignorance which Jesus, as light, has overcome (1:5; 16:33). The world thus hates Jesus and his followers (15:18–19; 17:14), rejoices over Jesus' departure/death (16:20) and remains in ignorance of the Father (17:25). Insofar as the world is governed by the devil (16:11) and rejects Jesus and the Spirit of truth (14:16–17), it is excluded from the blessings Jesus requests of his Father for his disciples (17:9, 16–17). However, these blessings are given so that the world might yet believe that the Father has sent Jesus (17:20–21). After Jesus' departure from the world, his disciples are promised protection, joy and fellowship with the Father and the Son (17:11, 13, 20–21). The disciples' responsibility in the world is to obey God's word as mediated through Jesus (17:6, 8, 14); to bring glory to Jesus (17:10); and to live in love for one another as they receive the love the Father has for them in Christ (17:23).

In the great prayer, Jesus addresses his Father as both holy and righteous (17:11, 25). The role of God as Father has defined Jesus' authority, identity and mission in John's gospel. The Father is primarily presented as the sender of the Son, and knowing and believing this is vital (17:3, 8, 18, 21, 23, 25). He is also portrayed as the lover (17:23–24, 26), the giver (17:2, 4, 6–7, 9, 11–12, 22, 24) and the sanctifier (17:17). Our reward will be to be with Jesus and to see his glory (17:24). It will not prove possible for us to play our part in the cosmic conflict which pervades Jesus' prayer unless we know his Father to be ours also (1 John 3:1–3).

4 Pilate and the soldiers

John 18:28—19:24

Pilate represented Caesar in Judea, and Roman imperium was required to carry out the Sanhedrin's capital verdict. However, Jesus is no helpless pawn in the power struggle that ensues between Pilate and the Jewish leaders; the theme of his kingship, which is a recurring motif in this episode, emphasises this very point. Some see Pilate's going back and forth between 'the Jews' and Jesus as symbolic of his vacillation and weakness. However, Pilate understood just how far it was worth pushing his authority and did not shirk from making politically expedient decisions when necessary. 'The Jews' may have felt they had successfully manipulated Pilate, but it cost them an acknowledgement of their subservience to Rome (19:15). Pilate reasserts his authority by his insistence on the wording of the *titulus*, which was deliberately calculated to humiliate and offend them, while unwittingly declaring the truth of this gospel (19:19–22; 1:49; 12:13).

The exchanges between Pilate and Jesus are revealing. Jesus accepts the premise that he is a king but defines this in terms of his coming to bear witness to the truth (18:37; an unusual Christmas text). Interestingly, a peculiarity of Pilate's question in Latin, '*Quid est veritas?*' ('What is truth?'), is that its anagram yields the answer: '*Vir est qui adest*' ('It is the man who is here'). Pilate's judicial role is to establish the truth, but even his unjust actions serve to establish Jesus' innocence for the reader. No wonder Pilate becomes more afraid and this fear elicits from him the leading question of John's gospel, 'Where do you come from?' (19:8–9). Jesus has already given his answer (18:36) and chooses instead to emphasise that Pilate is answerable to a higher power (19:11). Again Pilate fails at a critical juncture and chooses expedience as 'the Jews' play their final political trump card (19:12).

Thus Pilate enters the creeds as he consigns Jesus to the executioners. It was all in a day's work for these soldiers, but even these details serve to demonstrate that all has gone to a much higher plan as scripture is fulfilled through their actions (19:24). Sometimes we are tempted to ask the question 'Who is in control?', but we ought not to do so lightly and not wait patiently for an answer.

5 Mary Magdalene and Thomas

John 20

Mary Magdalene is almost the last character to be introduced in John's gospel (19:25). However, she serves as the disciple par excellence who was not only present at the cross but was also obedient to the first command of the risen Jesus (vv. 17–18). In many ways she illustrates the intertextual journey of the disciples' grief turning into joy (16:19–22). Her grief is evident in her distress and weeping over not knowing what has happened to Jesus' body (vv. 2, 13) and her confusion about the identity of the 'gardener' (v. 15). Note that Jesus reveals himself to Mary in stages. First he asks a quintessential Johannine question, 'Whom are you seeking?' (v. 15; see Jesus' first words in 1:38, which is a virtually identical question in Greek). But it is only when he speaks her name that she recognises Jesus' voice (v. 16; see 10:3–4) and her grief is turned to joy. Much is made of her holding on to Jesus and his prohibition, but the emotional character of this encounter and the need to make haste to tell the others seems enough to account for the nuances (v. 17).

Thomas, however, was late to the party (v. 24), but is the epithet 'doubting Thomas' fully deserved? His previous interventions illustrate other aspects of his character. He is faithful and decisive in his willingness to go with Jesus to his death (11:16), and while he is portrayed as questioning he seems eager for an answer (14:5). Yes, Jesus does tell him to stop doubting and believe, but what a believer he becomes (v. 28)! After all, Thomas was only asking for the same level of proof that the others had received, but his confession of faith exceeds all others. The only other place in John's gospel where Jesus is directly called God is in the very first verse (albeit as 'the Word'). For a Jew to confess such things, standing before the risen Jesus, forms an astonishing climax.

The theme of faith and sight runs like a thread through this chapter. Mary's devotion to Jesus and Thomas' confession of faith are to be our devotion and confession also. Yet we are blessed even though we have not seen as they have (vv. 29–31). If Jesus is anything less than 'Lord' (v. 18) and 'God' (v. 28), then to worship him is a form of idolatry.

6 The beloved disciple and Simon Peter

From the last supper onwards, except at Golgotha, Simon Peter and the disciple whom Jesus loved appear together almost like Siamese twins. However, it would be a mistake to conclude that they are portrayed as rivals. It is true that the beloved disciple is shown as being closer to Jesus than Peter (13:23–25); nearer to Jesus than Peter in the high priest's courtyard (18:15–16); more faithful than Peter in not abandoning Jesus at Golgotha, where he is also entrusted with responsibility for Jesus' mother (19:25–27); and faster than Peter in running to the empty tomb (20:3–4). Furthermore, he is more perceptive than Peter both at the tomb (20:8) and concerning the significance of the catch of fish in the boat (vv. 6–7). Finally, the beloved disciple is already said to be 'following' Jesus, while Peter is specifically commanded (twice!) to follow Jesus (vv. 19–20, 22). At every turn it could be said that the beloved disciple outclassed Peter in the discipleship stakes.

This is partly what may lie behind Peter's question about the beloved disciple, 'Lord, what about this man?' (v. 21). Will this disciple, perhaps more 'deserving', continue to be favoured in some way? This seems to be borne out in the text in which Peter is asked three times whether he loved Jesus (vv. 15–17), whereas this other disciple is described twice as the one whom Jesus loved (vv. 7, 20). But such comparisons, especially when we are confronted by our own sense of unworthiness, are invidious. Certainly, Peter has had to face his failures, and remarkably his own desire to lay down his life for Jesus will be fulfilled, but only on Jesus' terms (vv. 18–19). Jesus' reply reveals that such concerns are not for Peter (or any other disciple) to worry about (v. 22).

The path of following Jesus is not served by any sense of competitiveness, for our various callings are best fulfilled when they are viewed as complementary. Peter's calling is to be the shepherd and everything he has learned about himself will equip him for this task. The beloved disciple's calling is to be the witness of all these things. His closeness to Jesus and his perceptiveness are what make his witness credible (v. 24). Take time to thank the Lord for their differing contributions and for one other gifted Christian whom you admire.

Guidelines

John's gospel ends with a statement of purpose of the writing (20:30–31) and a guarantee of the veracity and integrity of the writer (21:24). Both statements speak of the many things to do with Jesus that had to be excluded. We can conclude from this observation that something or someone does not have to be known exhaustively in order to be known truly. The truth as it is in Jesus (14:6; Ephesians 4:21) is revealed in John's gospel in the way in which the divine glory is communicated in the fleshly existence of the Word (1:14a) and that this has been perceived through the human senses (1:14b; 1 John 1:1–4). This is the *spiritual mystery* of the incarnation.

We now know things about Jesus that could not possibly be true of any other human being. If Jesus says and does things that only God has the prerogative to say and do (and this is the basis of his conflict with the religious authorities), then it would be obdurate *not* to respond to Jesus as Thomas did (20:28). The significant themes of the gospel are revealed through the interactions *this* Jesus had with otherwise insignificant people (even Pilate would only warrant a small footnote in history). The universal has been encountered in the ordinary and the particular. This is the *intellectual scandal* of the incarnation.

John's gospel aims both to evoke faith in Jesus and to encourage faithful following of Jesus. Its witness is the inspiration for our witness to him before the watching world. Our understanding and experience of reading this gospel is thus only the prelude to our service and witness in the name of Jesus the Messiah, the Son of God, through which incredibly we can bring glory to him (17:10). This is the *practical consequence* of the incarnation for disciples of Jesus. Someone put it simply in verse like this:

You are writing a gospel, a chapter each day,
By the things that you do and the things that you say;
We read what you write, distorted or true.
What is the gospel according to you?

Do others hear of and see Jesus in our face-to-face encounters with them?

FURTHER READING

Cornelis Bennema, *Encountering Jesus: Character studies in the gospel of John* (Fortress Press, 2014).

Walking with the Judges: justice and mercy in the promised land

Isabelle Hamley

Judges is a little-loved book in the Bible. It seems strange, alien: characters are deeply flawed, violence and horror abound, and God often seems absent. Yet this book that seems so remote is deeply contemporary too: it deals with questions of leadership and the use and misuse of power, collective and individual responsibility, justice and mercy, gender relations, sexual and child abuse, individualism, greed, oppression, powerlessness… The themes are ones we recognise all too easily from today's headlines. So how can we read Judges in ways that enable us to attend to the presence of God in the midst of the messiness and pain of real life?

A number of arcs in the book help us do this. First, Judges is part of the 'Former Prophets' in the canon: this means it was intended to speak into the life of Israel, to challenge the people and make them think about their present. Reading Judges therefore isn't about simply mining history, or trying to find nuggets of teaching, but about listening to its challenge to the ways we live. Second, we find a clue in the name – 'Judges'. The Hebrew root translated as 'judges', *shophet*, also forms part of the Hebrew word for 'justice', *mishpat*, used repeatedly in the Old Testament in the encouragement to justice and righteousness. Judges is concerned with justice in the broadest sense; building a life that leaves behind the ways of thinking of Egypt and instead practises the ways of the Lord as outlined in the covenant in Sinai. The people find it hard! Judges explores the many forces that shape how we behave as communities and individuals, and how our behaviours and experiences shape communities where justice flourishes – or not.

We will look at Judges 1—9 in this two weeks of notes, and the remaining chapters in a subsequent issue of *Guidelines*.

Unless otherwise stated, Bible quotations are taken from the NRSV.

1 After the death of Joshua

Judges 1:1-26

It is easy to look back on the opening of Judges and assume that Israel must be on a high: God has delivered them from Egypt, Joshua has led a successful military campaign, the land is lying open before them, God is with them! The book of Joshua ended on a hopeful note, with a renewal of the covenant at Shechem. The reality of their situation, however, is not quite so rosy. They are a fairly small band of bedraggled refugees, with little to their name, few skills in battle, a band of people supposedly united by Yahweh but with little else to hold them together. As early as chapter 1 we see that they are not even one ethnic group but that others, like Caleb and Othniel the Kenizzites, have been welcomed in through faith. In a largely agricultural society, land meant survival. Unless the people could settle, they would die. The land, however, is occupied by the Canaanites, grouped around fortified cities, who have better technology, equipment and skills in war.

Israel is faced with a choice: do you trust in Yahweh, who brought their ancestors out of Egypt and promised to be with them – but who cannot be bought or manipulated and whose ways in war do not rely on human skill and planning but on obedience? Or do you fight your enemies on their own terms? The people waver.

There are three windows on to Israel's choices in Judges 1. First, they treat Adoni-Bezek in exactly the way he treats his enemies: with cruelty, maiming and shaming, rather than putting him to death as the law required. They choose to wage war with the tools of the local oppressive ruler. Does the end justify the means? Second, we have a much more hopeful window on to Achsah: as a woman, she is named, safe, speaks for herself, crosses the country on her own and brokers an inheritance for herself and her family by demanding sources of water, essential to survival in an agrarian society. Her family represent Judah, even though they are not ethnically Israelite: it is faith that has drawn them into the covenant. Finally, the house of Joseph chooses to make a forbidden and unnecessary covenant with the inhabitants of the land: they do not invite them to trust in Yahweh, do not fight them, but simply choose to cohabit. Israel's temptation is to settle the land on their own terms, rather than trust in Yahweh's.

2 A new life in a new land

Chapter 2 introduces themes that shape the whole of Judges. First, we see the difficulties of transmitting faith. One generation had experienced the leadership of Yahweh for themselves, and followed Joshua, a wise and discerning leader. The problem is, what next? How do you help a new generation have faith for themselves? The text is really interesting; on the one hand, the people had been given clear instructions to pass down the generations about how to live well with Yahweh and with one another. Deuteronomy has many commands relating to forming children into 'the ways of the Lord' through story and ritual, in family and community. Yet another generation, who had not seen (v. 6) or known (v. 10) what Yahweh had done, arises. The older generation may have failed to tell the story; but the new generation has a responsibility, and a task too. They need to come to know Yahweh for themselves. There is an experiential component to faith: it cannot just be handed down; it needs to be appropriated and lived in a new way for a new time. The way Israel had lived under Joshua needed adapting to new life as a settled, rather than a nomadic, community.

Second, we are introduced to a cycle of behaviour that will shape the rest of the book. The people sin – they 'do what is right in their own eyes'; sin here is an attitude that puts the self, the individual, at the centre of moral decision-making. Instead of doing what is right in Yahweh's eyes, human beings make themselves judges of good and evil, echoing Genesis 2. The catastrophic consequences of relative, individualised ethics and morality will unfold throughout the rest of Judges. As a result of their sin, Yahweh's presence withdraws, and they become who they are, a small people unable to resist the Canaanites' stronger force, who fall into bondage and oppression again. Then they cry out, and Yahweh raises up a judge, who delivers them. They do not even 'cry out' to Yahweh; a lot of the time, they simply groan in pain, without repentance or reflection on how their own actions have contributed to their situation. But Yahweh responds anyway. Strict justice would have left them to their own devices. But the heart of Yahweh's relationship to Israel is not mechanical consequences; it is compassion and mercy, a radical departure from the logic of Egypt and an invitation into a new way of being in the world.

3 Ehud: the James Bond of the Old Testament

Judges 3:12-30

Judges 3 gives us the first detailed window on to the life of one of Israel's leaders, Ehud. The cycle of behaviour is establishing itself. Israel sins, they suffer at the hand of their enemies and cry out, and God raises a deliverer. Ehud is an unexpected deliverer – and indeed, there is little to suggest he is even recognised as Yahweh's deliverer until he takes command of the troops. He is unexpected, because he is from Benjamin, a smaller tribe, and a left-handed (or possibly ambidextrous) man; being left-handed was regarded with suspicion at best in the ancient world. Ehud comes across as a loner, gaining entry to the palace and carrying out a covert mission, capitalising on the ineptitude of the oppressors.

The story is full of grim irony, written to show Israel's enemies as stupid, overfed and indulgent; as such, it is a typical story by an oppressed people trying to reassert themselves. It is also a story that exposes the dynamics of oppression. Eglon profits from the oppression of others: he and his generals are 'fat', while Israel suffers and has to bring 'tribute' that takes away from their own ability to flourish. Eglon is oblivious to the impact of his behaviour, and neither he nor his attendants consider the possibility that one, lone, oppressed Hebrew may rise against him. His behaviour as a ruler renders the true person in front of him invisible. The writer, meanwhile, turns Eglon into a caricature of a ruler, so that we see Israel and Moab locked in a dynamic of neither 'seeing' or acknowledging the other.

Ehud executes his plan. Nowhere does the text suggest that the plan had come from Yahweh, or was even necessary to victory. Ehud was raised as a deliverer, but it is not clear that the murder of Eglon was part of Yahweh's deliverance – though the degree of luck needed for success certainly suggests divine involvement. The narrator never makes Yahweh's intentions or actions explicit, beyond the choice of Ehud. Did Ehud behave rightly? Was the level of violence justified? Is the fate of Eglon 'justice'? Judges rarely answers the questions prompted by the narrative directly. Instead, it invites readers on a journey through the complexity of real life, with mixed human motives, questionable actions and the constant thread of divine presence throughout it all. And readers have to think, and pray, and consider the rest of scripture as they wrestle with the text.

4 Deborah and Barak: collaborative leadership

The cycle resumes in chapter 4, after a period of rest for the land. Despite the fact that Israel has moved away from the covenant and is oppressed and needs rescuing, there are still signs of hope. Deborah is a recognised prophetess, whose wisdom is well-known, so that many come to her for 'judgements', very likely judicial decisions on local disputes. Just like with Achsah, here, at the beginning of Judges, women are safe, independent and known by name. Deborah is even a religious leader, something that no other judge seems to undertake.

She is also a leader who does not seek to extend her reach or power. In traditional prophetic fashion, she hears from Yahweh and obeys. She invites a new leader for Israel to step up. Barak responds to the call as many others do; like Moses, he insists on the divine presence at his side. Deborah has spoken to him in the voice of Yahweh ('I will draw out Sisera…'). When Barak answers, 'If you go…', it is unclear whether 'you' is Yahweh, Deborah or both. As a prophet, Deborah would have symbolised the presence of God. Barak's demand therefore shows his acceptance that it is Yahweh who leads and gives victory, and humility about his own role. Yahweh is commander-in-chief and speaks through his prophet Deborah. Barak works with her, without trying to take over her role or hear directly from Yahweh. Both Barak and Deborah respond to their particular call, and they work together in response.

Deborah's response in verse 9 may be slightly odd. Is she irked that Barak wants her to come? Is she warning him? In a deeply patriarchal society, Barak's decision to let a woman be the mouthpiece of Yahweh, giving him and, by extension, his troops orders, would have inevitably raised eyebrows and diminished his status. Deborah's words remind him of the cost of the decision to obey. Barak is not swayed – following Yahweh matters more than his own status or glory. In this, he contrasts sharply with leaders to come. Gideon, Jephthah and Samson will all be keen to claim victory for themselves and to assert their own role in achieving it. Barak instead recognises that victory against 'all the chariots', the symbols of Canaanite superiority, can only be achieved through trust and obedience. Deborah and Barak together still evidence the covenantal attitude that Joshua had embodied, and they offer a rare positive example of humble and collaborative leadership.

5 Unexpected help

Judges 4:11–24

Chariots matter in Judges. They symbolise everything that the Canaanites have and Israel lacks: a complex, advanced society with technological know-how and settled life in prosperous cities. They also symbolise the oppression that local kings visit on others, exploiting them to increase their wealth and status. In this story, the chariots are mentioned again and again – Sisera assembles all his troops, all his chariots. The entire might of the Canaanite army is mustered against a small, trembling Israel, in a David-and-Goliath moment. The insistence suggests that there is no way out unless Yahweh intervenes – and indeed, it is Yahweh himself who vanquishes all the chariots (v. 15). Sisera then flees and abandons his own chariot, symbolically relinquishing his superiority and trust in human strength.

However, he has not yet shed his assumptions about himself. He still sees himself as important and expects others to serve and respect him, as a leader, a man, a warrior, a Canaanite. Like Eglon, he fails to see the person in front of him and the danger they may pose. He arrives at Heber's camp; the Kenites had a long association with Israel, sometimes their allies, sometimes not. Sisera, however, relies on a treaty between Heber and Jabin. He does not consider the possibility of split loyalties, nor does he consider that a woman may not share her husband's political choices or may be capable of violence.

Jael, meanwhile, is caught in an impossible situation. Refusing Jabin may put her at risk of immediate violence and jeopardise her husband's treaty. Inviting him in, when the Hebrews clearly have the upper hand, risks catastrophic retaliation from the advancing army. No window is given on to Jael's thoughts and feelings. She simply acts and takes a warrior's crown – the life of the enemy general. Symbolically, she becomes deliverer of Israel: a non-Israelite, female, nomadic saviour, as unexpected as can be. In the world of ancient warfare, she takes the glory, as Deborah had predicted a woman would.

The story therefore does not split leadership and deliverance just two ways, but three, with each participant unexpected in some way. Yahweh does not restrict himself to working with armies and human skills, but widens the circle beyond expected male leaders to women and outsiders of Israel itself. The motif of the inclusion of the stranger within the work of Yahweh follows from Achsah and Caleb earlier, and forms a strong counterpoint to the command to annihilate the other.

6 Praise and the formation of community

Chapter 5 retells the story in Deborah's own words, in the biblical tradition of victory songs, like those of Moses and Miriam, praising God for his actions. Such songs are an essential part of community and faith formation: they commit the story of Yahweh's actions to memory; they interpret and theologise the story, so that the community and their descendants are formed in discerning how Yahweh works within their history. The song also delineates the contours of Israel as a nation and how it relates to others – friend and foe – and therefore shapes Israel's social identity at a time when who Israel is remains fluid (we can see this fluidity by the fact that the list of tribes keeps changing, and the boundaries of which ethnic groups are in are porous).

Having two versions of one story also helps us ask penetrating questions, by noticing the gaps between the reliable narrator's version and the more stylised, poetic characters' version. Yahweh takes centre-stage in deliverance in both, so that the unified message is one that encourages Israel to trust Yahweh and abide by the covenant. Two aspects of the song, however, raise interesting questions.

First, the retelling of the Jael episode is far more violent, enhanced by poetic repetitions and rhythm, and Jael is presented as more powerful as Sisera is never portrayed asleep. Together with lengthy description of the mustering of Israelite troops, it suggests a tendency to glorify violence and war skills that was not present in the narrative. Second, the glimpse of Sisera's mother shows the vulnerability of women in war, liable to be seized by men as war captives to be raped and abused. Sisera's mother fantasises about the fate of Hebrew women, while readers know that their fates may soon be reversed. Neither Deborah nor Sisera's mother, however, shows compassion towards the other: ethnic solidarity wins over gender. These aspects of the song problematise the violence and general war culture of Israel. Are they really different from the Canaanites? The final verse captures the ambiguity, by calling a curse on Yahweh's enemies and blessing on Yahweh's friends.

The entire story of Judges is that of Israel turning away from Yahweh's friendship, yet Yahweh responds with grace. Israel's imagination is shaped by a retributive rhetoric rather than a theology of grace, and the people fail to see themselves as they are before God.

Guidelines

The book of Judges opens with stories of real humanity: not perfect heroes, not a perfect people and not a perfect relationship with God. Instead, a mixed picture emerges, a truthful rather than a doctored picture of the complexity of living as God's people. In these opening chapters, we see glimpses of hope and glory and the start of a downward spiral into sin and moving further and further away from Yahweh. Yet right from the start, the presence and patience of God shine through. God works with his people as they are, not as they should be, which brings a mix of judgement and grace, as God maintains his covenantal promise of caring for Israel, even when Israel walks away.

The questions faced by the people resonate today, too.

- A clear conundrum for the people is how to enable their descendants to live as people of the covenant. How do we form the next generation in the ways of the Lord? How do we enable faith to move from head knowledge to personal experience? One of the ways the Israelites did this was through the retelling of their story; think through how you tell your story and that of your community.

- The relationship between Yahweh and his people is never based on a purely mechanical or retributive process; instead, it is shaped by love and compassion. How do we respond to those who fail? To ourselves, when we fail? How do we hold together justice and mercy?

- How far are we shaped by those who surround us? Israel quickly takes on the surrounding nations' approach to justice, judgement, war and violence. What are your perspectives on these questions shaped by? And how would you go about developing a deeper Christian imagination?

29 August–4 September

1 The call of Gideon

Judges 6:1–24

The state of Israel is worse than ever before. They hide in caves, their crops and livestock destroyed, and they are attacked by enemies as thick as locusts: the picture reminds us of Egypt, except that now it is Israel who suffers from the plagues. They cry out in pain, but this time Yahweh sends a prophet.

Unlike Deborah, this prophet is unnamed, unknown and unheeded. No response is forthcoming from Israel. They cry out for deliverance but are unwilling to examine themselves for their own part in their misfortune and work towards change.

Yahweh still cares, however, so he sends an angel to call Gideon to action. The story works as a call narrative, similar to Moses and various prophets. The angel's opening address, 'you mighty warrior', is somewhat ironic, given Gideon is hiding from enemies and performing a domestic task. The greeting is a traditional assurance of God's presence, something which Gideon is unsure about and which he counters with a challenge. He can see little evidence of the presence of Yahweh. Even though the greeting was for him alone, he makes no distinction between Yahweh being with him or the people as a whole. Gideon seems to assume that 'God with him' means extraordinary miracles or great historical deeds, rather than a daily presence in covenant relationship. In addition, Gideon blames Yahweh for his absence and does not see that it is Israel that has walked away from Yahweh.

Gideon protests some more when told he is to deliver Israel, and he demands some form of assurance. This will be a key motif in his story; Gideon is logical and assesses rational evidence around him. First, he judges circumstances as evidence of the absence of God; then he offers food and sees what the angel does; later, he will set tests. Gideon wavers constantly between belief and disbelief, between faith and doubt, between trust and fear. Fear and presence are interwoven throughout the story. The remedy to fear in the Old Testament is never great deeds or supernatural deliverance; it is the assurance 'I am with you'. Gideon is struggling with a recurrent question for people of faith: the desire to control God's response, to understand it or anticipate it. Instead, what God invites him to do, as with Moses and Joshua before him, is to trust in his presence: that is, to rely on the relationship between them rather than mechanical patterns of help.

2 A testing time

Judges 6:25–40

Gideon has glimpsed the presence of God and built an altar in 6:24, but we now find out that Gideon's father sponsors Baal worship, with a different altar at the heart of the village. The two altars graphically illustrate the state of Israel, a state that needs remedying. Yahweh therefore tasks Gideon with replacing

Baal's altar with Yahweh's. In other words, Gideon will have to declare himself for Yahweh and against Baal. He cannot simply be a military deliverer but must call the people back to God and attribute his leadership to Yahweh's actions. There is to be no doubt that it is God who delivers.

Gideon is, understandably, afraid, and sets out to destroy the pagan altar at night. The fact that his father sponsors the local cult, and that he has ten servants to himself, suggests that Gideon may not be as insignificant as he had claimed to the angel in 6:15 and shows him as less vulnerable than first thought. Nevertheless, the destruction of the altar and the added injury of building a new altar, to a different God, and offering a sacrifice using the wood of the sacred pole, provokes anger as expected. Gideon's father rises to defend his son and, unwittingly, asks a profound theological question. Do men need to defend their God? Shouldn't their God fight for themselves? The rest of the narrative shows that Yahweh delivers his people, while Baal needs defending by those who worship him. Idols are revealed to be worthless, and the people's tendency to think of their gods in very human terms is exposed.

Yet despite his apparent victory, Gideon still doubts. God had tested him; now Gideon tests God. The well-known story of the fleece is not a story of Gideon seeking the mind or will of God. He already knows what God's will is – he has been told! Gideon may doubt his own ability to listen or he may doubt Yahweh's word; alternatively, he may still wonder whether he has made the right choice in Yahweh over Baal. Baal was a weather god, in particular associated with dew. To ask Yahweh to perform a dew miracle is to ask him to show he is more potent than Baal. Gideon resists faith and trust; he wants certainty. Extraordinarily, Yahweh obliges. He does not berate Gideon for his lack of faith or refuse to give proof. Instead, Yahweh walks patiently with Gideon as Gideon's incipient faith grows.

3 For Yahweh and Gideon

Judges 7

Gideon is now ready. Troops are mustered, Yahweh on his side and Gideon probably expects that war and victory will swiftly follow. God, however, intervenes unexpectedly. Troops are too numerous! For Gideon, who started out somewhat timid and unsure he wanted to fight, or whether Yahweh was as powerful as Baal, this must be crushing. All his preparation, all his skill with a sword, all the skill of the people gathered around him – none of this is meant to give him victory. Gideon has, quite understandably, trusted in numbers and practical preparations. Yahweh instead wants him to trust in God alone.

This is not just about trust, however. A people consistently victorious on the battlefield against the odds could quickly become warlike and abuse their power to start empire-building. Here, they fight for survival, but Yahweh's directions, as commander-in-chief, aim to prevent them from thinking too much of themselves, seeking to dominate others around them or glorify warrior culture. The army is sifted down to a fraction of its size. First, those who are afraid are released, which is ironic given that Gideon himself will need reassuring of Yahweh's presence yet again. Gideon chooses not to admit his own vulnerability or weakness. Second, the men who stay are chosen based on drinking posture – that is, on random, arbitrary criteria rather than skill or valour. The army is completely Yahweh's army, and Gideon struggles to trust.

Yahweh again shows himself as patient and kind towards his creatures. Gideon has not asked for a sign, but God knows he is afraid and takes the initiative. Gideon has to admit that he is afraid first: learning honesty with God is part of the journey of faith and the reshaping of a culture of war and masculinity that had become too similar to Canaan's. It is the enemy's dream and interpretation that reassures Gideon. Using the enemy shows Yahweh's power over everything; he is not merely a tribal god who cares about Israel only, as ancient Near Eastern gods were often imagined to be. He is God over the weather and over the enemy.

Gideon is now ready – and his confidence brims over. As he leads the troops into battle, his war cry, 'For the Lord and for Gideon!', rings ominously. Is he putting himself on a par with God? Is he claiming victory for himself? Is he using the opportunity to gather allegiance for himself?

4 Things fall apart

Judges 8:4–28

Gideon's newfound confidence swiftly turns to arrogance – and his leadership from God-given to self-seeking. He didn't send all the dismissed troops home, but they stood by and now join in pursuing the fleeing enemy. No divine command sends them in pursuit; this is entirely Gideon's doing. His war cry signalled his unwillingness to attribute victory to Yahweh alone or to let God direct the battle in its entirety. Now Gideon wants the trophy of capturing the enemy kings.

29 August–4 September

The incident in Succoth and Penuel reveals a ruthless side to Gideon. He now has power and wields it to get his way. When his compatriots resist, doubting that he will gain victory, he shows neither patience nor kindness towards them, but treats them with disproportionate brutality. The first Israelites to die violently in Judges die at the hand of one of their own. The events will inspire fear in others, so that they will respect and obey Gideon. It takes practically no time for Gideon to taste power and grasp it for himself.

The motif of the misuse of power threads itself throughout the Old Testament, in many forms and contexts. Power in itself is not wrong; God himself appoints leaders to ensure good order and work towards the common good. Their power, however, is limited by the laws of the covenant, which prevent the accumulation of riches and inherited privilege. Gideon does not heed the laws – he amasses wealth, land and a harem, and promotes a local pagan cult like the king-priests of surrounding nations. He started well, destroying the altar of Baal, but ultimately holding on to his power becomes more important than holding on to the covenant.

Exodus and Deuteronomy repeatedly highlight the danger of coming into power after liberation, with the injunction, 'Do not forget that you were once slaves/aliens.' As the people settle in the promised land, their greatest challenge is to let their imaginations be transformed: away from the coercive power of Egypt, away from its use and abuse of human beings for the sake of the privileged few, away from the greedy grasp of empire. Yahweh's dealings with Israel, based on compassion, embody a different way of being, one that will come to its full expression in the gospels' accounts of Jesus' relinquishing of divine power. But for now, Israel's imagination is still captive, and they make Gideon into a ruler indistinguishable from those of the surrounding nations.

5 The rise of Abimelech

Judges 9:1–25

Judges so far has had many leaders, from the lone, independent Ehud, to Deborah and Barak's cooperation, to Gideon's overbearing leadership. As Gideon ages, he consolidates his position into one very close to that of local kings and fathers many children, including one outside of his polygamous marriages, setting the scene for a family feud.

Scripture does not prescribe any model of political organisation over another one. Rather, it explores the pitfalls and limits of leadership, the importance of character in leaders and the ultimate failure of leadership that is not based on a transformed covenantal relationship with Yahweh. Here, in the story of Abimelech, the exploration of how communities organise themselves widens and includes mutual responsibility between leader and people, so that leaders are not held solely responsible for the fate of a community and for their use of power, but are rather shown as part of a holistic system where those who give them leadership share in accountability for their choice of leader.

Leadership and its impact are not considered simply in the public arena; the increasing length of each judge's story reveals complex individuals shaped by their parents' actions and by their early experiences, and whose private lives shape their public responses and choices. Equally, the impact of leadership on ordinary Israelites becomes clearer: first with Gideon's sponsoring of a pagan cult, now with Abimelech's kingship causing fear within Israel and returning the highways to a state of danger that had been the mark of pre-deliverance Israel in Deborah and Gideon's stories. In many ways, Abimelech's impact is closer to that of an oppressor.

Abimelech's background as a child who somehow does not quite fit into his family dramatically shapes his actions; so do his father's choices. Gideon behaved like a king and called his son from a concubine Abimelech, that is, 'my father is king'. The boy was caught between the promise of his name and the reality of his birth. The impact of parents on their children is a theme that stretches back as far as Isaac and Jacob's stories in Genesis. Human beings are not shaped by their own choices and decisions only, but by the community that surrounds them, so that sin affects each new generation in continuity with the previous one. How each person responds to their past, and the offer of transformation and new life through partnership with God, is a key strand of biblical portraits of real, flawed human beings.

6 The bramble king

Judges 9:26–57

The first part of the story of Abimelech featured the parable of Jotham, a tale that warns that people get the leaders they deserve and that an unworthy leader will unleash destruction through fire on to those around him. The second part of Abimelech's story makes the parable come true, lending Jotham's words a prophetic edge.

Abimelech, supposedly king of Shechem, does not live where he reigns, but has installed a steward, Zebul, who reports seditious talk from Shechem's elite. Abimelech does not try to negotiate, ascertain facts or seek a peaceful solution. Instead, he attacks, as he attacked and killed his brothers to gain power, and more Israelites are killed by one of their own. Shechem had been the place where the covenant had been renewed at the end of Joshua, and was the location of the first Passover in the promised land. Now it is a town of unclear allegiance, with a pagan temple that financed Abimelech's rise to power, used as refuge by the 'lords' of the town. Abimelech first kills the men and women who come out early to work in the fields, likely to be poorer and of lesser status; then he moves into the city. The local elite, meanwhile, do not defend the city they are supposed to rule and represent, but flee to safety for themselves. The pattern establishing itself here is one of chaos and anarchy, within which the most vulnerable members of society get hurt first. Neither Abimelech nor other leaders seek the common good. Instead, Abimelech acts out of vengeful spite and the 'lords' out of self-preservation. True to the fable, bad leaders fail their people and fire comes out of Abimelech, the 'bramble king', to destroy all.

Once Abimelech starts, he cannot stop, and he turns to attack another city, unprovoked, for no reason. There, all the inhabitants take refuge together – including a poor woman with a handheld millstone, a symbol of basic agrarian work. Abimelech fails to see the difference and repeats his tactics, though his ends are unclear: he is laying waste to his own kingdom. In the end, Abimelech, who killed his 70 brothers on one stone to achieve status and fame, is killed by one stone, from the unnamed woman, who delivers her people from Abimelech's oppression. There is a sense of poetic justice in the death, yet also of utter devastation. Israel's failure to heed covenantal principles destroys the community leaders are meant to nurture.

Guidelines

This second week of readings from Judges establishes a pattern of increasing deterioration in Israel. Not only do the people return to sin and forget Yahweh, but the leaders also become an integral part of the problem, rather than the solution. The community, turning away from Yahweh and the guidelines set in the covenant for Israel to flourish, is a source of chaos; yet Israel's problems are not limited to the choices of each current generation. Each new generation is shaped by the one that came before, and carries the wounds and hurts of the past in ways that distort their present. Yahweh's response of justice and mercy becomes increasingly needed: how could justice be just, if it did not include mercy for the ways in which people and community are shaped by their past and experiences? Yet how can mercy not include justice, if the future is to be better than the present?

The stories of Gideon and Abimelech lay open the complexity of our responses as human beings, the ways in which our choices are often a mix of free will and being shaped by other forces. They also stress the importance of collective accountability, so that scapegoating of leaders cannot become an easy way out of examining everyone's part in difficult times. Yet they also remind us that God ultimately works with these mixed and messy realities: when Gideon owns his fear and acknowledges it, Yahweh responds in grace and gentleness. The same offer is open today.

- How do we become aware of how our experiences have shaped us, and what vulnerabilities and strengths they may have created?
- How do we discern wisely how to act in and shape our communities – whether communities of faith or wider communities?
- How do we hold together justice and mercy in our interpersonal relationships?

FURTHER READING

Robert Alter, *Ancient Israel: The former prophets: Joshua, Judges, Samuel and Kings* (W.W. Norton & Co, 2013).

Mercedes L. García Bachmann, *Wisdom Commentary: Judges* (Liturgical Press, 2018).

Daniel I. Block, *The New American Commentary: An exegetical and theological exposition of holy scripture: Judges, Ruth – Vol. 6* (B&H Publishing Group, 1999).

Barry G. Webb, *The New International Commentary on the Old Testament: The book of Judges* (William. B. Eerdmans, 2012).

Become a Friend of BRF
and give regularly
to support our ministry

We help people of all ages to grow in faith

We encourage and support individual Christians and churches as they
serve and resource the changing spiritual needs of communities today.

Through **Anna Chaplaincy**
we're enabling churches to provide
spiritual care to older people

Through **Living Faith**
we're nurturing faith and resourcing
life-long discipleship

Through **Messy Church**
we're helping churches to reach out
to families

Through **Parenting for Faith**
we're supporting parents as they raise
their children in the Christian faith

Our ministry is only possible because of the generous support of
individuals, churches, trusts and gifts in wills.

As we look to the future and make plans, **regular donations make a huge
difference** in ensuring we can both start and finish projects well.

By becoming a Friend of BRF and giving regularly to our ministry you are
partnering with us in the gospel and helping change lives.

How your gift makes a difference

£2
a month

Helps us to develop **Living Faith** resources to use in care homes and communities

£10
a month

Helps us to support churches running the **Parenting for Faith** course and stand alongside parents

£5
a month

Helps us to support **Messy Church** volunteers and resource and grow the wider network

£20
a month

Helps us to resource **Anna Chaplaincy** and improve spiritual care for older people

 # How to become a Friend of BRF

Set up a Direct Debit donation at **brf.org.uk/donate** or find out how to set up a Standing Order at **brf.org.uk/friends**

Contact the fundraising team

Email: **giving@brf.org.uk**
Tel: +44 (0)1235 462305
Post: Fundraising team, BRF, 15 The Chambers, Vineyard, Abingdon OX14 3FE

Good to know

If you have any questions, or if you want to change your regular donation or stop giving in the future, do get in touch.

Registered with

FR

FUNDRAISING
REGULATOR

SHARING OUR VISION – MAKING A ONE-OFF GIFT

I would like to make a donation to support BRF.
Please use my gift for:

☐ Where it is most needed   ☐ Anna Chaplaincy   ☐ Living Faith

☐ Messy Church   ☐ Parenting for Faith

Title	First name/initials	Surname
Address		
		Postcode
Email		
Telephone		
Signature		Date

Our ministry is only possible because of the generous support of individuals, churches, trusts and gifts in wills.

giftaid it   You can add an extra 25p to every £1 you give.

Please treat as Gift Aid donations all qualifying gifts of money made

☐ today,   ☐ in the past four years,   ☐ and in the future.

I am a UK taxpayer and understand that if I pay less Income Tax and/or Capital Gains Tax in the current tax year than the amount of Gift Aid claimed on all my donations, it is my responsibility to pay any difference.

☐ My donation does not qualify for Gift Aid.

Please notify BRF if you want to cancel this Gift Aid declaration, change your name or home address, or no longer pay sufficient tax on your income and/or capital gains.

Please complete other side of form

SHARING OUR VISION – MAKING A ONE-OFF GIFT

Please accept my gift of:

☐ £2 ☐ £5 ☐ £10 ☐ £20 Other £ [   ]

by (*delete as appropriate*):

☐ Cheque/Charity Voucher payable to 'BRF'

☐ MasterCard/Visa/Debit card/Charity card

Name on card

Card no. [   ] [   ] [   ] [   ]

Expires end [M M] [Y Y]   Security code* [   ]

*Last 3 digits on the reverse of the card
ESSENTIAL IN ORDER TO PROCESS
YOUR PAYMENT

Signature   Date

☐ I would like to leave a gift to BRF in my will.
Please send me further information.

For help or advice regarding making a gift, please contact
our fundraising team +44 (0)1865 462305

Your privacy

We will use your personal data to process this transaction.
From time to time we may send you information about
the work of BRF that we think may be of interest to you.
Our privacy policy is available at **brf.org.uk/privacy**.
Please contact us if you wish to discuss your mailing
preferences.

Registered with

(FR)

FUNDRAISING
REGULATOR

↩ Please complete other side of form

Please return this form to 'Freepost BRF'
No other address information or stamp is needed

Bible Reading Fellowship is a charity (233280) and company limited by guarantee (301324),
registered in England and Wales

GL0222

Guidelines forthcoming issue

Like the chocolates behind the doors of an Advent calendar, we have a lot of treats in store for us in the upcoming issue of *Guidelines*.

First, we have the continuation of two fantastic series that started in this issue. Ashley Hibbard will finish off her notes on the Joseph cycle, as the story shifts focus from Joseph himself to his brothers and how they react to Joseph's tests. And Steve Walton takes us through the second letter to the Christians at Thessalonica, written perhaps only a few weeks after the first, with its focus on suffering, false teaching and internal tensions within the church.

As we reach the final months of 2022, we finish our series on life's milestones. Kate Bruce gives us an intriguing series on childhood, and how we nurture, protect and form potential in the next generation, while also learning from them. At the opposite end of life, Henry Wansbrough provides a week on life after death, including some fascinating readings taken from the Apocrypha.

For Advent itself, we have two slightly more unusual series. Matthew Knell looks at the unexpected advents of Christ, to shake us out of our familiarity with certain biblical texts and to help us to experience them alongside those who were originally present. Meanwhile, Imogen Ball takes us through the season by looking at that much-loved Advent hymn, 'O come, O come, Emmanuel', examining the biblical basis for each verse and how they lead us towards rejoicing.

Alongside these, we have a challenging series on Amos from Peter Hatton and a provocative series on James from Rosalee Velloso Ewell. David Spriggs looks at twin parables – those that appear in pairs – and Phil Grasham, who wrote helpful notes on honour and shame previously, is writing for us again, this time on cross-cultural insights into scripture.

Finally, Ruth Bancewicz from The Faraday Institute for Science and Religion brings us a unique series about our planet and God as creator of the whole earth. Each reflection in this series is written by a different scientist from the institute. Ultimately, it encourages us to acknowledge our dependence on God and draws us into worship of him – as should all the notes.

What the Bible means to me: Rachel Tranter

The Bible, for me, is the way that I discover who God is.

The Bible is full of stories of people – mostly ordinary, every-day human beings – encountering God in so many different ways. The ways that they encounter God mirror the myriad ways that Christians around the world discover God today. For some, this experience is dramatic and full of power. For others, it's gentle.

The Bible is the same: powerful and gentle. It can challenge, provoke, upset and empower. It can also comfort, reassure, refresh and invigorate. To some extent, it only has this impact on us as we let it – that is, let the Holy Spirit.

That's because the Bible is not just a signpost towards God; it is also infused with God in the person of the Holy Spirit. The Bible without the Holy Spirit is just a book. It can only truly reveal God to us as we open our hearts to the Spirit – and only then can we mine the depths of its treasures in ways that truly transform us.

I am currently studying for an MA in Mission, as well as working as Editorial Manager for BRF and editing *Guidelines*. All of these make great use of the Bible, to the extent that sometimes it can feel transactional. I can read a stunning piece of scripture and life-changing reflections on it – and simply move on, because there are things to do and places to be. Whenever I read the Bible – whether devotionally or as part of my work or study – I need to let it and the Holy Spirit into my heart, not just my head.

I encourage you to do the same.

Recommended reading

In *Grief Notes* Tony Horsfall charts the first year of his grief journey since the death of his wife from cancer. Month by month he tells the unfolding story of walking with and through loss, weaving this together with biblical teaching on grief and insights gained from grief counselling. With a poignant mix of honesty and humour, Tony shares the challenges of rebuilding his life and reflects on how he has seen God meet his needs as he wrestled with grieving in a time of lockdown and pandemic. The following is an edited extract taken from the first chapter of the book.

Grief Notes
Walking through loss
The first year after bereavement

Tony Horsfall

13 July

Evelyn passed away peacefully in the early hours of this morning. I had prayed with her last night before I left Cherry Trees, the care home where she was being nursed. Although at that stage she was not able to communicate much, at the end of my prayer she blurted out, 'Thank you, Jesus. You led me all the way.' These were the last words she spoke, and they gave me great assurance that she was ready to go home to be with Jesus.

The care home called me just after 2.00 am, but when I got there, she was gone. It was hard to see her lying there, lifeless, her skin cold and the colour of bone china. Even though expected, her death was still a shock. I packed her things and tidied her room as I waited for the undertaker to arrive. I spoke to my son Alistair in Australia, as I knew he would be awake.

Then, with great dignity, she was taken away, and I was alone. I will never see her again on this earth.

A time for everything

You may be familiar with the great passage in Ecclesiastes 3:1–11 with its 14 statements about life, realities that are as true now as when they were when first written centuries before Christ was born. It begins like this: 'There is a time for everything, and a season for every activity under the heavens' (v. 1). Then comes the first punch line, describing the most universal of life experiences, and it hits you hard in the stomach – 'A time to be born and a time to die' (v. 2). In a culture that likes to pretend that death is not real and can be avoided, we are pierced by the raw reality that there will come a moment in time when death touches every one of us.

Death is inevitable. There is a time to be born. There is a time to die. No-one lives for ever, and sooner or later we will become familiar with the reality that we – and those we love – are frail and finite creatures with a limited timespan on planet earth. We can celebrate births and birthdays with joy and gladness, but inevitably we shall also mourn the death of loved ones and grieve their passing with tears of sadness.

Grieving is painful, for as we read here there is also a time to weep (v. 4). Of course, we would prefer life to be all sunshine, every day filled with fun and laughter, but the shadow of death is never far away, especially as we get older. Grief is the price we pay for loving, and our tears reflect the pain we feel when we lose someone dear to us.

Grief is not permanent, however. We may never completely get over it, but we do come through it. 'There is a time to mourn and a time to dance' (v. 4). It may seem impossible when we are in the midst of grief to think that we could ever be happy again, but we will be. Slowly, with the passing of time and the brave work that grieving well requires of us, we will emerge into the brightness of a new day. Joy will return. That has to be our hope, for without such a prospect we may well stay submerged in the darkness of loss forever.

This truth gives us belief that we can find a way through our grief and come out the other side to live again. Yes, and even to dance once more!

To order a copy of this book, please use the order form on page 151 or visit **brfonline.org.uk**.

The Bible is at the heart of BRF's work, and this special anniversary collection is a celebration of the Bible for BRF's centenary year. Bringing together a fantastically wide-ranging writing team of authors, supporters and well-wishers from all areas of BRF's work, this resource is designed to help us go deeper into the story of the Bible and reflect on how we can share it in our everyday lives.

The BRF Book of 365 Bible Reflections
with contributions from BRF authors, supporters and well-wishers
978 1 80039 100 0 £14.99
brfonline.org.uk

The People's Bible Commentary
The Gospels and Acts
John Proctor, Dick France, Henry Wansbrough,
Richard A. Burridge and Loveday Alexander
978 1 80039 093 5 £39.99
brfonline.org.uk

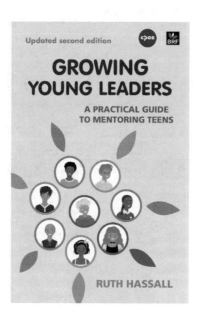

Growing Young Leaders offers practical guidance for all those mentoring 13- to 18-year-olds in a faith context, with a view to nurturing them towards leadership roles. It defines mentoring, analyses the necessary skills and attributes of a mentor today, encourages good practice, considers the safeguards needed to meet child protection guidelines and, above all, considers how to help young people identify their gifts and grow as Christian disciples.

Growing Young Leaders
A practical guide to mentoring teens
Ruth Hassall
978 1 80039 128 4 £8.99
brfonline.org.uk

To order

Online: brfonline.org.uk
Telephone: +44 (0)1865 319700
Mon–Fri 9.30–17.00

Delivery times within the UK are
normally 15 working days. Prices are
correct at the time of going to press
but may change without prior notice.

Title	Price	Qty	Total
Grief Notes	£8.99		
The BRF Book of 365 Bible Reflections	£14.99		
The People's Bible Commentary: The Gospels and Acts	£39.99		
Growing Young Leaders	£8.99		

POSTAGE AND PACKING CHARGES			
Order value	UK	Europe	Rest of world
Under £7.00	£2.00		
£7.00–£29.99	£3.00	Available on request	Available on request
£30.00 and over	FREE		

Total value of books	
Donation*	
Postage and packing	
Total for this order	

* Please complete and return the
Gift Aid declaration on page 141.

Please complete in BLOCK CAPITALS

Title _____ First name/initials _____ Surname _____

Address _____

_____ Postcode _____

Acc. No. _____ Telephone _____

Email _____

Method of payment

☐ Cheque (made payable to BRF) ☐ MasterCard / Visa

Card no. ☐☐☐☐ ☐☐☐☐ ☐☐☐☐ ☐☐☐☐

Expires end ☐☐ ☐☐ Security code ☐☐☐ Last 3 digits on the reverse of the card

We will use your personal data to process this order. From time to time we may send you information
about the work of BRF. Please contact us if you wish to discuss your mailing preferences **brf.org.uk/privacy**

Please return this form to:

BRF, 15 The Chambers, Vineyard, Abingdon OX14 3FE | **enquiries@brf.org.uk**

For terms and cancellation information, please visit **brfonline.org.uk/terms**.

BRF needs you!

If you're one of our regular *Guidelines* readers, you will know all about the benefits and blessings of regular Bible study and the value of serious daily notes to guide, inform and challenge you.

Here are some recent comments from *Guidelines* readers:

'... very thoughtful and spiritually helpful. [These notes] are speaking to the church as it is today, and therefore to Christians like us who live in today's world.'

'You have assembled an amazingly diverse group of people and their contributions are most certainly thoughtful.'

If you have similarly positive things to say about *Guidelines*, would you be willing to share your experience with others? Could you ask for a brief slot during church notices or write a short piece for your church magazine or website? Do you belong to groups, formal or informal, academic or professional, where you could share your experience of using *Guidelines* and encourage others to try them?

It doesn't need to be complicated: just answering these three questions in what you say or write will get your message across:

- How do *Guidelines* Bible study notes help you grow in knowledge and faith?
- Where, when and how do you use them?
- What would you say to people who haven't yet tried them?

We can supply further information if you need it and would love to hear about it if you do give a talk or write an article.

For more information:

- Email **enquiries@brf.org.uk**
- Telephone BRF on +44 (0)1865 319700 Mon–Fri 9.30–17.00
- Write to us at BRF, 15 The Chambers, Vineyard, Abingdon OX14 3FE

Enabling all ages to grow in faith

At BRF, we long for people of all ages to grow in faith and understanding of the Bible. That's what all our work as a charity is about.

- Our **Living Faith** range of resources helps Christians go deeper in their understanding of scripture, in prayer and in their walk with God. Our conferences and events bring people together to share this journey, while our Holy Habits initiative helps whole congregations grow together as disciples of Jesus, living out and sharing their faith.

- We also want to make it easier for local churches to engage effectively in ministry and mission – by helping them bring new families into a growing relationship with God through **Messy Church** or by supporting churches as they nurture the spiritual life of older people through **Anna Chaplaincy**.

- Our **Parenting for Faith** team coaches parents and others to raise God-connected children and teens, and enables churches to fully support them.

Do you share our vision?

Though a significant proportion of BRF's funding is generated through our charitable activities, we are dependent on the generous support of individuals, churches and charitable trusts.

If you share our vision, would you help us to enable even more people of all ages to grow in faith? Your prayers and financial support are vital for the work that we do. You could:

- Support BRF's ministry with a regular donation;
- Support us with a one-off gift;
- Consider leaving a gift to BRF in your will (see page 154);
- Encourage your church to support BRF as part of your church's giving to home mission – perhaps focusing on a specific ministry or programme;
- Most important of all, support BRF with your prayers.

Donate at **brf.org.uk/donate** or use the form on pages 141–42.

One size fits all?

For just as the body is one and has many members, and all the members of the body, though many, are one body, so it is with Christ. For in one Spirit we were all baptised into one body.

1 CORINTHIANS 12:12 (ESV)

Trying to make something that works for everyone is an immensely difficult task – ask anyone who has ever tried to plan a group holiday! Throw that out to the entire world – we know that people are wonderfully and remarkably different and we change so much throughout our lives as well. From babies to children to adults to older people, everyone is spectacularly unique.

Our mission as a charity is to encourage all people of all ages to grow in their faith. We share the message of God's love for the world in many different ways, because we know that a one-size-fits-all approach doesn't work with the profoundly varied world our God created.

From our Living Faith team creating Bible reading notes for individuals, like the ones you are holding now, to our Parenting for Faith team working to empower parents to raise God-connected children and teenagers. From our Messy Church team resourcing and equipping leaders to run church that reaches out to families to our Anna Chaplaincy team sustaining those working with older people, combatting loneliness and bringing comfort.

We're always looking for new ways to help people grow in faith as well as ways to reach more people with the things we do. Our work is only possible because of generous donations from individuals, charitable trusts and gifts in wills. If you would like to help us make what we do possible through a regular gift, find out how to give at **brf.org.uk/friends** or get in touch with our fundraising team on 01235 462305 or via **giving@brf.org.uk**.

Your prayers, as ever, are hugely appreciated.

Judith Moore
Fundraising development officer

Give. Pray. Get involved.
brf.org.uk

GUIDELINES SUBSCRIPTION RATES

Please note our new subscription rates, current until 30 April 2023:

Individual subscriptions
covering 3 issues for under 5 copies, payable in advance
(including postage & packing):

	UK	Europe	Rest of world
Guidelines 1-year subscription	£18.30	£26.25	£30.15
Guidelines 3-year subscription (9 issues)	£53.55	N/A	N/A

Group subscriptions
covering 3 issues for 5 copies or more, sent to one UK address (post free):

Guidelines 1-year subscription	£14.55 per set of 3 issues p.a.

Please note that the annual billing period for group subscriptions runs from 1 May to 30 April.

Overseas group subscription rates
Available on request. Please email **enquiries@brf.org.uk**.

Copies may also be obtained from Christian bookshops:

Guidelines	£4.85 per copy

All our Bible reading notes can be ordered online
by visiting **brfonline.org.uk/subscriptions**

Guidelines is also available as
an app for Android, iPhone and iPad
brfonline.org.uk/apps

All our Bible reading notes can be ordered online by visiting
brfonline.org.uk/subscriptions

Title _____ First name/initials _____ Surname _____

Address _____

_____ Postcode _____

Telephone _____ Email _____

Please send *Guidelines* beginning with the September 2022 / January 2023 /
May 2023 issue (*delete as appropriate*):

(*please tick box*)	UK	Europe	Rest of world
Guidelines 1-year subscription	☐ £18.30	☐ £26.25	☐ £30.15
Guidelines 3-year subscription	☐ £53.55	N/A	N/A

Optional donation to support the work of BRF £ _____

Total enclosed £ _____ (cheques should be made payable to 'BRF')

Please complete and return the Gift Aid declaration on page 141 to make your
donation even more valuable to us.

Please charge my MasterCard / Visa with £ _____

Card no. ☐☐☐☐ ☐☐☐☐ ☐☐☐☐ ☐☐☐☐

Expires end [M][M] [Y][Y]   Security code ☐☐☐   Last 3 digits on the reverse
of the card

To set up a Direct Debit, please complete the Direct Debit instruction on page 159.

Please return this form to:
BRF, 15 The Chambers, Vineyard, Abingdon OX14 3FE

For terms and cancellation information, please visit **brfonline.org.uk/terms**.

Bible Reading Fellowship is a charity (233280) and company limited by guarantee (301324),
registered in England and Wales

GL0222

GUIDELINES GIFT SUBSCRIPTION FORM

☐ I would like to give a gift subscription (please provide both names and addresses):

Title _____ First name/initials _____ Surname _____

Address _____

_____ Postcode _____

Telephone _____ Email _____

Gift subscription name _____

Gift subscription address _____

_____ Postcode _____

Gift message (20 words max. or include your own gift card):

_____

_____

Please send *Guidelines* beginning with the September 2022 / January 2023 / May 2023 issue *(delete as appropriate)*:

(please tick box)	UK	Europe	Rest of world
Guidelines 1-year subscription	☐ £18.30	☐ £26.25	☐ £30.15
Guidelines 3-year subscription	☐ £53.55	N/A	N/A

Optional donation to support the work of BRF £ _____

Total enclosed £ _____ (cheques should be made payable to 'BRF')

Please complete and return the Gift Aid declaration on page 141 to make your donation even more valuable to us.

Please charge my MasterCard / Visa with £ _____

Card no. ☐☐☐☐ ☐☐☐☐ ☐☐☐☐ ☐☐☐☐

Expires end ☐☐ ☐☐ Security code ☐☐☐ Last 3 digits on the reverse of the card

To set up a Direct Debit, please complete the Direct Debit instruction on page 159.

Please return this form to:
BRF, 15 The Chambers, Vineyard, Abingdon OX14 3FE

For terms and cancellation information, please **visit brfonline.org.uk/terms**.

Bible Reading Fellowship is a charity (233280) and company limited by guarantee (301324), registered in England and Wales

You can pay for your annual subscription to our Bible reading notes using Direct Debit. You need only give your bank details once, and the payment is made automatically every year until you cancel it. If you would like to pay by Direct Debit, please use the form opposite, entering your BRF account number under 'Reference number'.

You are fully covered by the Direct Debit Guarantee:

The Direct Debit Guarantee

- This Guarantee is offered by all banks and building societies that accept instructions to pay Direct Debits.
- If there are any changes to the amount, date or frequency of your Direct Debit, Bible Reading Fellowship will notify you 10 working days in advance of your account being debited or as otherwise agreed. If you request Bible Reading Fellowship to collect a payment, confirmation of the amount and date will be given to you at the time of the request.
- If an error is made in the payment of your Direct Debit, by Bible Reading Fellowship or your bank or building society, you are entitled to a full and immediate refund of the amount paid from your bank or building society.
- If you receive a refund you are not entitled to, you must pay it back when Bible Reading Fellowship asks you to.
- You can cancel a Direct Debit at any time by simply contacting your bank or building society. Written confirmation may be required. Please also notify us.

Instruction to your bank or building society to pay by Direct Debit

Please fill in the whole form using a ballpoint pen and return with order form to:
BRF, 15 The Chambers, Vineyard, Abingdon OX14 3FE

Service User Number: | 5 | 5 | 8 | 2 | 2 | 9 |

Name and full postal address of your bank or building society

To: The Manager	Bank/Building Society
Address	
	Postcode

Name(s) of account holder(s)

Branch sort code

Bank/Building Society account number

Reference number

Instruction to your Bank/Building Society
Please pay Bible Reading Fellowship Direct Debits from the account detailed
in this instruction, subject to the safeguards assured by the Direct Debit Guarantee.
I understand that this instruction may remain with Bible Reading Fellowship
and, if so, details will be passed electronically to my bank/building society.

Signature(s)

Banks and Building Societies may not accept Direct Debit instructions for some
types of account.

Enabling all ages to grow in faith

Anna Chaplaincy

Living Faith

Messy Church

Parenting for Faith

100 years of BRF

2022 is BRF's 100th anniversary! Look out for details of our special new centenary resources, a beautiful centenary rose and an online thanksgiving service that we hope you'll attend. This centenary year we're focusing on sharing the story of BRF, the story of the Bible – and we hope you'll share your stories of faith with us too.

Find out more at **brf.org.uk/centenary**.

To find out more about our work, visit
brf.org.uk

Sharing *the* Story *since* 1922